# ANTHOLOGY OF CLASSICAL PIANO MUSIC

### Intermediate to Early Advanced Works by 27 Composers

## EDITED BY MAURICE HINSON

Cover art:  Detail from An Architect's Table, *1772*
*Thomas-Germain-Joseph Duvivier (French, 1735–1814)*
*Oil on canvas, 40 3/8 x 31 in.*
*Norton Simon Art Foundation, Pasadena, California*

# ANTHOLOGY OF CLASSICAL PIANO MUSIC

## EDITED BY MAURICE HINSON

## Contents

Foreword: The Classical Period (1750–1820) . . . . . 4

Ornamentation . . . . . . . . 5

About This Edition . . . . . . 6

Suggested Further Reading . . . . . . . 7

Acknowledgments. . . . . . 7

About the Composers and the Music . . . . . . . . . . . . . . . . . 8

ANGLÉS, RAFAEL

Sonata in F Major . . . . . . . . . . . . . . . . . . . . . . . . . . . . 23

BEETHOVEN, LUDWIG VAN

Bagatelle in D Major, Op. 119, No. 3 . . . . . . . . . . . . . . 26

Bagatelle in C Major, Op. 119, No. 8 . . . . . . . . . . . . . . 28

Bagatelle in F Major, Op. 33, No. 3 . . . . . . . . . . . . . . 29

Bagatelle in G Major, Op. 126, No. 1 . . . . . . . . . . . . 32

Country Dance in C Major, WoO 14, No. 1 . . . . . . . . . 34

Country Dance in E-flat Major, WoO 14, No. 7 . . . . . . 35

Für Elise, WoO 59 . . . . . . . . . . . . . . . . . . . . . . . . . . 36

Six Easy Variations on an Original Theme, WoO 77 . . . . 40

Six Écossaises, WoO 83. . . . . . . . . . . . . . . . . . . . . . . 48

Sonata in G Minor ("Easy Sonata"), Op. 49, No. 1 . . . . . 54

BENDA, GEORG ANTON

Sonatina in D Major. . . . . . . . . . . . . . . . . . . . . . . . . . 68

CIMAROSA, DOMENICO

Sonata in B-flat Major . . . . . . . . . . . . . . . . . . . . . . . 71

CLEMENTI, MUZIO

Preludio alla Haydn, Op. 19, No. 2 . . . . . . . . . . . . . . . 74

Sonatina in G Major, Op. 36, No. 5 . . . . . . . . . . . . . . 77

Waltz in F Major, Op. 39, No. 4 . . . . . . . . . . . . . . . . . 89

DITTERSDORF, CARL DITTERS VON

Three English Dances. . . . . . . . . . . . . . . . . . . . . . . . . 92

DUSSEK, JAN LADISLAV

Polonaise in F Major, Op. 16, No. 6 . . . . . . . . . . . . . . 94

DE GAMBARINI, ELISABETTA

Three Dances

Minuet . . . . . . . . . . . . . . . . . . . . . . . . . . . . . . . . . 96

Tempo di Gavotta . . . . . . . . . . . . . . . . . . . . . . . . . . 97

Giga . . . . . . . . . . . . . . . . . . . . . . . . . . . . . . . . . . . 98

HÄSSLER, JOHANN WILHELM

Etude No. 5 in B-flat Major, Op. 49, No. 5 . . . . . . . . . 100

Etude No. 6 in B-flat Minor, Op. 49, No. 6 . . . . . . . . . 101

Two Scottish Dances. . . . . . . . . . . . . . . . . . . . . . . . . 102

HAYDN, FRANZ JOSEPH

Scherzo in F Major, Hob. XVI:9 . . . . . . . . . . . . . . . . . 104

Sonata in E Major, Hob. XVI:13 . . . . . . . . . . . . . . . . 105

Sonata in E Minor, Hob. XVI:34 . . . . . . . . . . . . . . . . 114

HAYDN, MICHAEL

Polonaise in C Major. . . . . . . . . . . . . . . . . . . . . . . . . 129

Theme with Variations . . . . . . . . . . . . . . . . . . . . . . . . 130

HEWITT, JAMES

    *Mark My Alford* . . . . . . . . . . . . . . . . . . . . . . . . . . . 132

HOFFMEISTER, FRANZ ANTON

    *Menuettino* . . . . . . . . . . . . . . . . . . . . . . . . . . . . . . 140

HUMMEL, JOHANN NEPOMUK

    *Gigue in D Major* . . . . . . . . . . . . . . . . . . . . . . . . . . 142

    *Menuet in C Major*, Op. 42, No. 3 . . . . . . . . . . . . . 143

KUHLAU, FRIEDRICH

    *Six Variations*, Op. 42, No. 1 . . . . . . . . . . . . . . . . . 146

MOZART, WOLFGANG AMADEUS

    *Adagio in B Minor*, K. 540 . . . . . . . . . . . . . . . . . . . 149

    *Klavierstück in F Major*, K. 33B . . . . . . . . . . . . . . . 155

    *Two Contredanses in G Major*, K. 269B, Nos. 1 and 2 . . 156

    *Fantasy in D Minor*, K. 397 . . . . . . . . . . . . . . . . . . 159

    *Sonata in A Minor*, K. 310 . . . . . . . . . . . . . . . . . . . 166

MYSLIVEČEK, JOSEF

    *Divertimento No. 6 in C Major* . . . . . . . . . . . . . . . . 190

NEEFE, CHRISTIAN GOTTLOB

    *Toccata in D Minor* . . . . . . . . . . . . . . . . . . . . . . . . 193

PLEYEL, IGNAZ JOSEPH

    *Minuet in C Major* . . . . . . . . . . . . . . . . . . . . . . . . 198

    *Rondo in G Major* . . . . . . . . . . . . . . . . . . . . . . . . . 200

REICHARDT, JOHANN FRIEDRICH

    *Prelude in C Major* . . . . . . . . . . . . . . . . . . . . . . . . 202

REINAGLE, ALEXANDER

    *Steer Her Up and Had Her Gawn* . . . . . . . . . . . . . . . . 203

RIES, FERDINAND

    *Trifle*, Op. 58, No. 12 . . . . . . . . . . . . . . . . . . . . . . 207

SCHUBERT, FRANZ

    *Five Écossaises* . . . . . . . . . . . . . . . . . . . . . . . . . . . 210

    *Two Ländler*, D. 366, Nos. 3 and 4 . . . . . . . . . . . . 213

    *German Dance in C Major*, D. 41, No. 20 . . . . . . . . 214

    *Hungarian Melody*, D. 817 . . . . . . . . . . . . . . . . . . 216

    *Impromptu in A-flat Major*, Op. 142, No. 2; D. 935 . . . 220

    *March in B Minor* (no Deutsch number) . . . . . . . . . . 226

    *Moments musicaux*, Op. 94, Nos. 3 and 6; D. 780

        *No. 3 in F Minor* . . . . . . . . . . . . . . . . . . . . . . 229

        *No. 6 in A-flat Major* . . . . . . . . . . . . . . . . . . . 231

TAYLOR, RAYNOR

    *Rondo in G Major* . . . . . . . . . . . . . . . . . . . . . . . . . 234

TÜRK, DANIEL GOTTLOB

    *Sonatina in F Major* . . . . . . . . . . . . . . . . . . . . . . . 238

WEBER, CARL MARIA VON

    *Three Écossaises* . . . . . . . . . . . . . . . . . . . . . . . . . . 241

WESLEY, SAMUEL

    *Prelude in A Major* . . . . . . . . . . . . . . . . . . . . . . . . 244

    *Sonata in B-flat Major*, Op. 5, No. 2 . . . . . . . . . . . 246

This volume is dedicated to Dr. William Phemister, with admiration and appreciation.

*Maurice Hinson*

# Foreword:
## The Classical Period (1750–1820)

The Classical period falls between the Baroque (1590–1750) and the Romantic (ca. 1820–1910) periods. Characteristics of Classical style are balance, elegance, simplicity, contrast, clarity and restraint. The terms *classical* and *classic* frequently refer to a standard or model of excellence, one of enduring value.[1] In music, the term *classical* is used more for quick reference than a detailed description, for works that have stood the test of time.

English music historian Charles Burney (1726–1814), in his *General History of Music* (1789), attributed the beginning of what we call the Classical style to the generation of composers who appeared in Naples, Italy around 1720. Burney identified the basic characteristics of the Classical style as homophonic texture and simple flowing melodies. Other components are the development of strong period structure (two- and four-measure phrases); more use of affections and style contrast within the pieces, use of crescendos and diminuendos, varied rhythms and strong tonic-dominant harmony. Elements of the Classical style appear in Italy around 1730 with the use of early sonata form.

Another important element that helped shape Classical style was the shift, around 1750, of the musical amateur public's attention from the violin to the keyboard instrument played by one performer.

The variety of style characteristics of the period from around 1720 to 1765 has suggested use of the term "Pre-Classical," an early period before the "pure" classicism of Franz Joseph Haydn (1732–1809) and Wolfgang Amadeus Mozart (1756–1791). Another name for this period is *Rococo*.

"Early Classical" style was known as *style galant*, which referred to the free or homophonic style as opposed to the German tradition (contrapuntal and polyphonic style) of the first half of the 18th century. Characteristics of the *galant* style include a lightness of texture, periodic phrasing with predictable cadences, ornamented airy melodies, simple harmonies, and an elegant sentimentality. This style was the main style of the early Classical period.

The term *galant* suggested what was contemporary, fashionable and in good taste. If a man possessed these qualities, he was referred to as *galant homme* (gallant man). Jean Antoine Watteau (1684–1721) used the term in his paintings known as *fêtes galantes*.

From approximately the 1760s until the end of the century the most characteristic forms became the sonata (sonata-allegro emphasizing the sections of exposition, development and recapitulation) and the rondo. The mature works of Haydn, Mozart and Muzio Clementi (1752–1832) are the pinnacle of this style.

The term "late Classical" is used for those who followed Haydn and Mozart, who generally paid more attention to motivic development. Ludwig van Beethoven (1770–1827) is best regarded as part Classical and part Romantic, straddling both the 18th and 19th centuries.

*Sturm und Drang* (storm and stress) was another movement during the Classical period that reached its zenith around the 1770s. This movement began in German literature but soon spread to other arts. Its aim was to overwhelm with emotion, to frighten, to stun—a very subjective approach to the arts emphasizing gut reactions rather than rational or logical thought. These characteristics are found in melodramatic works by Georg Anton Benda (1722–1795), operas and ballets by Christoph Willibald Gluck (1714–1787), Mozart's operas *Idomemeo* and *Don Giovanni*, plus Haydn's and Mozart's minor-key symphonies and some of their piano works.

The obvious starting point for a discussion of music from the Classical period is composition for solo keyboard, where a transformation of style, coinciding with the tendency of national styles to unite, is reflected in the rise of the piano and the decline of the harpsichord.

The very important Classical sonata idea (already briefly mentioned) was developed during this period. It employed the idea of contrasting a range of emotions in one piece. Many theories describe sonata form as an organized sequence of an exposition that included first subject, transition, second subject, closing theme, development and recapitulation, each with a "proper" key. This provides a handy framework, but this does not always stand up when it is carefully applied to the actual sonata movements of the composers in this collection. These great composers did not always have such a conscious plan in mind: the sonata principle was a constantly developing idea within which experimentation and adventure took place.

---

[1] Eugene K. Wolf in *The New Harvard Dictionary of Music* (Cambridge, MA: Harvard University Press, 1986), 172.

# Ornamentation

Ornamentation in the Classical period was very similar to the Baroque period but fewer different ornament signs were used.

Ornaments must be performed correctly in the style of the period. First, learn the pieces in this anthology without ornaments and then add them to fit properly with the melodic line. Many students are anxious about executing ornaments and play them too fast, as if to get them over as quickly as possible, and their fingers depress the keys too hard. Let the ornaments sing and try to transmit their character and quality into the fingers.

Even though the main ornaments are realized (notated) throughout this anthology, the following section realizes the most important ornaments used in the Classical period.

*1. Trill:*

Trills usually begin on the beat and usually start with the upper (auxiliary) note. The speed and number of repercussions of trills is at the player's discretion and is determined by the tempo, the character of the music and the time value of the note on which it occurs. The shortest trill would contain two repercussions. Trills should be played with uniform and rapid finger strokes. In the following instances, trills may begin on the main note rather than the upper (auxiliary) note:

a) when the trill is preceded by a small or normal sized note, one legato step above the main note.

b) in a continuous chain of trills such as:

c) sometimes to clarify the melodic line.

d) Franz Schubert's trills more often begin on the main note than the upper.

*2. Pralltriller (snapped trill, half trill or tied trill):*

The curved line is not a slur but a tie and is used only with a descending second. The three remaining notes should be played very quickly.

*3. Trill substitutes or quick notes:*

If the performer cannot play the full four notes for a trill or a quick note, a single appoggiatura may be substituted in its place today.

*4. Mordant:*

The mordant (from the Latin word *mordere,* meaning "to bite") moves in the opposite direction of the trill. It begins on the main note, on the beat, and alternates with the lower note ("bites it"). It should be played as quickly as possible. Short mordants contain only one repercussion. The long mordant contains two or more repercussions and comes to rest, like the short mordant, on the main note before the time value is completed.

*5. Turn:*

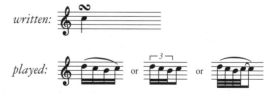

The turn uses both the upper and lower notes. When the turn is placed above its main note, the upper note is played on the beat and is followed by the main note, lower note and replayed main note. The notes may divide the time value of the main note evenly, or be played more quickly so that the last note is held.

The turn placed between main notes decorates the first one, after it has been played, in the following manner:

6. *Appoggiatura:*

The appoggiatura (leaning note) appears in music as a small note slurred to the main note. The appoggiatura is an accented dissonance and should be played on the beat, taking its value from the note that follows.

a) The long appoggiatura takes half the time of its main note.

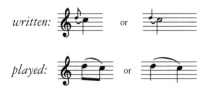

Long appoggiaturas may take two-thirds of the value of the main note if this main note is dotted (more easily divisible by three).

b) The short appoggiatura takes as little time as possible from the main note and is only ornamental. It frequently occurs before fast notes and must be played with great rapidity so that the main rhythmic outline remains.

In the Classical period, the symbol ♪ came into use. This was the old way of writing a sixteenth note ♪ and was eventually used to notate a sixteenth-note appoggiatura. Mozart was one of the first composers to notate appoggiaturas with this symbol. It should be played on the beat and given the value of a sixteenth-note. An additional flag was used to indicate the thirty-second-note appoggiatura ♪, which was used with sixteenth notes.

## About This Edition

*Anthology of Classical Piano Music* provides an up-to-date, comprehensive survey of piano music from the Classical period. It includes a variety of teaching repertoire, which has been selected to provide the widest range of styles and idioms from the period. Most of the music comes from the great masters, but a few worthy works from lesser-known composers are also included. The works range in difficulty from the intermediate to the early-advanced level.

All pieces are in their original form and nothing has been added or deleted unless mentioned in footnotes. In a few instances, single movements and selected pieces have been chosen from more lengthy works, a practice common during the Classical period.

This anthology is a performing edition. Brief discussions about the composers and music, history, performance problems and suggestions, along with the form of each piece, are presented in the section "About the Composers and the Music." Essential ornamentation is realized in footnotes. All fingerings are editorial unless stated otherwise. All parenthetical material is likewise editorial.

This volume has been prepared with piano performance in mind, utilizing all of the resources of the modern piano, with full appreciation of its tonal properties. All of the expressive qualities of the fortepiano are utilized as effectively as possible in the music originally written for this instrument. All pedal indications are editorial unless stated otherwise in footnotes. Editorial pedal has been added for the aid of students. More or less pedal than indicated can be used when playing these pieces.

## Suggested Further Reading

Badura-Skoda, Paul and Eva. *Interpreting Mozart on the Keyboard.* English trans. Leo Black. New York: St. Martin's Press, 1962.

Brown, Alfred Peter. *Joseph Haydn's Keyboard Music: Sources and Style.* Bloomington: Indiana University Press, 1986.

Clementi, Muzio. *Introduction to the Art of Playing on the Pianoforte.* London: Clementi, Banger, Hyde, Collard and Davis, 1801. Reprint, New York: Da Capo Press, 1973.

Czerny, Carl. *On the Proper Performance of All Beethoven's Works for the Piano.* English trans. Paul Badura-Skoda. Vienna: Universal Edition, 1963.

Newman, William. *The Sonata in the Classic Era.* Chapel Hill: University of North Carolina Press, 1963.

————. *Beethoven on Beethoven: Playing His Piano Music His Way.* New York: W. W. Norton, 1988.

## Acknowledgments

Thanks to editors E. L. Lancaster and Sharon Aaronson for their generous assistance and expert editorial advice.

# About the Composers and the Music

## RAFAEL ANGLÉS
### (ca. 1730–1816)

Anglés was born in Rafales, Spain. He was named first organist of Valencia Cathedral in 1762 where he remained for the rest of his life. Anglés composed music for keyboard and the church.

*Sonata in F Major* . . . . . . . . . . . . . . . . . . . . . . . . 23

Form: Binary. Part I = measures 1–32; Part II = 33–70.

This sonata is written in binary form and is lighter in texture and contrast than Padre Antonio Soler's (1729–1783) works. This sonata, as well as the other Anglés works, shows the influence of Franz Joseph Haydn. This piece contains a suggestion of Spanish dance rhythms. Keep the sound and touch light. Separate eighth and quarter notes and connect the sixteenths and thirty-seconds.

## LUDWIG VAN BEETHOVEN (1770–1827)

Beethoven was one of the world's greatest composers and an outstanding pianist. His early training was with his father and organist Christian Neefe (1748–1798). He studied briefly with Haydn (1732–1809) and after he moved to Vienna in 1792 he had lessons with Johann Schenk (1753–1836), Georg Albrechtsberger (1736–1809) and Antonio Salieri (1750–1825). He began to lose his hearing, was forced to give up playing in public by 1815 and total deafness set in by 1820. Before his death Beethoven was recognized as the greatest composer of his generation. He was a vital influence on all areas of instrumental composition throughout the 19th century.

*Bagatelle in D Major*, Op. 119, No. 3 . . . . . . . . . . 26

Form: **A** = measures 1–16; **B** = 16–32; **A** = 1–16; coda = 32–56.

*Bagatelle* literally means "trifle," but it seems more appropriate to translate it as little or small piece. Beethoven named his Opp. 33, 119 and 126 sets of piano pieces *Bagatelles*. With this form, sometimes called "character piece," Beethoven opened the door to a new form of expression. The bagatelle is a brief, concentrated work, usually in the ternary form of **A B A**, used to express contrasting subjects, i.e., the dramatic and the lyrical. The Op. 119 set of bagatelles was composed between 1820 and 1822. No. 3 *á l'Allemande* is written in the style of a German waltz. Accent beat 3 in the right hand in measures 2, 6, 10 and 14. Take plenty of time in measures 27–28 and 31–32; do not make the editorial staccatos too short. Vary dynamics on repeats.

*Bagatelle in C Major*, Op. 119, No. 8 . . . . . . . . . . 28

Form: Binary. Part I = measures 1–8; Part II = 9–20.

This gentle "minuet" is in two parts. The sudden change of harmony at measure 9 is characteristic of Beethoven in his later years. Legato is the key to a fine performance of this piece. A number of finger substitutions are required to maintain the proper smooth and connected style. Vary the dynamics on the repeats.

*Bagatelle in F Major*, Op. 33, No. 3 . . . . . . . . . . . 29

Form: **A** = measures 1–18; **B** = 18–33; **A**$^1$ = 34–65; coda (based on **B**) = 65–76

This piece is from a larger set of seven that were published in 1802. The *sf* in measures 1–2 and 10–12 are small accents while the ones in measures 14–15 are stronger accents (because of the *f* in measure 14). Play the short appoggiatura in measures 3, 7, 16, etc., on the beat. The shift of key from F major (measure 4) to D major (measure 5) is a special surprise. Beethoven uses this shift from F major several times.

*Bagatelle in G Major*, Op. 126, No. 1 . . . . . . . . . . 32

Form: Binary. Part I = measures 1–16; part II = 16–47.

The set of *Six Bagatelles*, Op. 126, of which this is the first, was the last work Beethoven composed for the piano. They were written at various times during 1823 and are, in their own way, as original and representative as anything Beethoven wrote in the last three or four years of his life. They are, if anything in music can be, self portraits, as they express his moods and frame of mind on the day he composed them.

No. 1 shows him to be in a songful (*cantabile*) and agreeable (*compiacevole*) mood. The lovely eight-measure melody (pickup to measure 1–8) is repeated in the pickup to measure 9–16 with variations. The second part (much longer than the first part) shows the melody being developed and by the meter change at measure 21 the even eighth notes are compressed into triplets, syncopated triplets, sixteenths, syncopated sixteenths and finally (after a short cadenza at measure 30) into high register figuration that closes the piece quietly. Beethoven reminds us (in addition to the double dots) that he wants the second part repeated (*La seconda parte due volte*). Begin the trills (in measure 9–10 and 29–30) on the principal note; the voice leading is more clearly heard.

## Country Dance in C Major, WoO 14, No. 1 . . . . . . 34

Form: Binary. Part I = measures 1–8; part II = 8–16.

This type of dance is of British origin. The performers stand opposite one another, as distinguished from a round dance. The term covers a whole series of figure dances that developed from dances on the English village green. This dance contains some delightful off-beat accents in measures 2 and 4.

## Country Dance in E-flat Major, WoO 14, No. 7 . . . 35

Form: Binary. Part I = measures 1–8; part II = 8–16.

Beethoven was very fond of this theme, as he used it in the Finale of the *Eroica Symphony* (No. III, Op. 55), in the *15 Variations and Fugue*, Op. 35 and for the ballet *The Creatures of Prometheus*. Be careful that the active left-hand sixteenth notes in measures 5–6 do not catch you by surprise. Aim for a big dynamic contrast between the chords in measures 10 and 12.

## Für Elise, WoO 59. . . . . . . . . . . . . . . . . . . . . . . . . . 36

Form: Rondo. **A** = measures 1–24; **B** = 24–39; **A** = 40–61; **C** = 62–83; **A** = 84–105.

This famous piece was composed in 1810 and is a rondo with two episodes. It is appropriate to play the left-hand accompaniment much quieter than the right-hand melody. Keep the right hand close to the keys with a legato touch, dropping and lifting the arm as phrases begin and end. The left hand should be light as a feather, brushing over the keys in graceful sweeps. For sustaining effect, the pedal should catch the notes being swept across. The pedal marks in measures 2–4, and 10–14 are Beethoven's and may reasonably be assumed to be applicable to all parallel passages. The pedal mark in measures 79–83 is also Beethoven's. Each broken chord supplies the necessary "filling in" to support the melody. One basic tempo should be maintained throughout the piece.

## Six Easy Variations on an Original Theme, WoO 77 . . . . . . . . . . . . . . . . . . . . . . . . . . . . . 40

Form: Theme and six variations plus coda.

This little masterwork was composed around 1800 and contains a most appealing theme in two parts (each repeated, measures 1–16). Be sure the melody is always clearly projected over the supporting harmonies.

**Variation I** contains the basic harmony with right-hand sixteenth figuration.

**Variation II** retains the harmony and turns the figuration into triplets. Connect sixteenth notes and separate eighth notes (unless indicated otherwise as in measure 43); quarter notes may also be separated.

**Variation III** alternates the melody in octaves while the other hand provides sixteenth-note accompaniment. In measures 55–56 (first half) and 71–72 the right hand is assigned two voices: both should be played legato.

**Variation IV** contrasts the two parts: measures 73–80 seem gloomy while the mood in measures 80 (second half) to 88 seems to become lighter. Most of this variation should be played legato.

**Variation V** flows with supple three-voice writing and colorful florid inner voices. This variation also requires mainly legato touch.

**Variation VI** is brilliant with all of the fleet thirty-second notes. The coda (measure 123 to the end) is ingenious by including varied parts of the theme.

## Six Écossaises, WoO 83 . . . . . . . . . . . . . . . . . . . . . . 48

Form: The six *écossaises* form a quasi-rondo when performed as a set. I (**A**) = measures 1–16, refrain = 17–32; II (**B**) = 1–16, refrain = 17–32; III (**C**) = measures 1–16, refrain = 17–32; IV (**D**) = measures 1–16, refrain 17–32; V (**E**) = measures 1–16, refrain = 17–32; VI (**F**) = measures 1–16, refrain = 17–32.

These vigorous and fun-to-play *écossaises* were possibly composed around 1806 and are probably piano transcriptions of orchestral dances. All six are in E-flat major since they collectively form one continuous composition. The second sixteen measures of the first *écossaise* (measures 17–32) serves as a refrain. Keep the tempo approximately the same in all parts with no interruption between the dances. The *écossaise* is a type of contredanse that was very popular in France in the late 18th century and was related to the British country dance. The origin of the name is a mystery since there appears to be nothing Scottish about the character of the music, which is written in a lively 2/4 meter. Separate quarter notes and connect eighth notes, unless indicated otherwise.

### *Sonata in G Minor* ("Easy Sonata"), Op. 49, No. 1 . . . 54

This sonata dates from around 1795–96, years that were especially productive for Beethoven. During this time he composed his first two piano concertos—the B-flat major (1795) and the C major (1795, revised in 1800).

**Andante.** Sonata form: Exposition = measures 1–33; development = 33–63; recapitulation = 64–102; coda = 103–110.

This melancholy-sounding movement should move in a flowing four beats to the measure rather than the indicated two. The three grace notes in measures 14 and 15 should be played on the beat. Arrive punctually at the *p* D in the right hand of measure 64, but then extend its length slightly before moving into the theme in tempo.

**Rondo—Allegro.** Rondo form: Main theme (**A**) = measures 1–16; episode in tonic minor (**B**) = 16–20; new theme (**C**) = 20–31; second group in B-flat (**D**) = 32–64; return to episode in G minor (**B**) = 64–68; recapitulation of episode theme (**C**) = 68–80; main theme (**A**) = 80–103; recapitulation of second group (**D**) = 103–135; coda = 135–164.

Keep the eighths in the opening leggiero (light) but slightly marcato (marked). Play the grace notes in measures 15–16 and similar places on the beat as acciaccaturas (crushed notes). Beginning at measure 32 the right-hand eighth notes should take on a more cantabile (singing) touch.

### GEORG ANTON BENDA (1722–1795)

Benda was a Bohemian composer whose compositions created a link between the late Baroque and Viennese Classical music. He was a close friend of C.P.E. Bach (1714–1788), whose influence can be seen in many of Benda's keyboard works, and he was greatly appreciated by Mozart. Benda wrote 34 piano sonatinas and at least 55 sonatas.

### *Sonatina in D Major* . . . . . . . . . . . . . . . . . . . . . . . 68

Form: Rondo. **A** = measure 1–12; **B** = 13–21; $A^1$ = 22–30; **C** = 30–40; $A^1$ = 41–50.

This delightful sonatina contains a strong dance influence. The sixteenth notes should be played legato and the eighth notes nonlegato, unless indicated otherwise. A short cadenza may be improvised and inserted in measure 22 at the fermata. Keep the entire piece light and sprightly.

### DOMENICO CIMAROSA (1749–1801)

This Italian composer worked in Naples and Rome and became one of the most successful opera composers of his generation. During 1787–91 he was chapel master in St. Petersburg for the Russian court and during 1791–93 he served in a similar post for the Austrian court in Vienna. He composed over 60 operas, sacred vocal music, over 80 keyboard sonatas, 9 harpsichord concertos and chamber works. His keyboard sonatas are thin-textured and homophonic. They use scale passages and broken-chord figuration in early Classic style, similar to the music of Domenico Scarlatti (1685–1757).

### *Sonata in B-flat Major* . . . . . . . . . . . . . . . . . . . . . 71

Form: Binary. Part I = measures 1–22; part II = 22–51.

This sonata exudes a cheerful mood. Connect sixteenth notes and separate eighth notes unless indicated otherwise. Project the left-hand parts that cross over the right hand at measures 11–12 and 39–40.

## MUZIO CLEMENTI (1752–1832)

Clementi was well known throughout his lifetime. Born in Italy, he was taken as a young lad to England to study. He became famous as a composer, keyboard performer, music publisher, teacher and manufacturer of pianofortes.

*Preludio alla Haydn*, Op. 19, No. 2 . . . . . . . . . . . . 74

Form: Two unequal parts. Part I = measures 1–33; part II = 33–46.

This piece is from a set of *Twelve Preludes* composed in the style of other composers written around 1787. Clementi even parodies himself in the final two preludes. Clementi seems to have had the first movement of Haydn's *Sonata in C Major*, Hob. XVI:35, in mind for this fantasy-like improvisational prelude. In measure 5 and similar places, play the right-hand sixteenth note with the last note of the triplet. Bring out the left-hand part in measures 12–14 (in measure 14 until the last half beat where the right hand takes over).

*Sonatina in G Major*, Op. 36, No. 5 . . . . . . . . . . . 77

This sonatina is from the sixth edition of these famous pieces. The sixth edition was published in 1820, 23 years after the first edition. Clementi taught these sonatinas over the years and constantly kept revising them. On the front page of the sixth edition is stated: "with considerable improvements by the author." The sixth edition contains many changes in the pieces, especially the use of higher octaves and thickening of the texture at certain places. Clementi also included pedaling in this edition. On page 8 of his *Introduction to the Art of Playing the Piano Forte* (1801) Clementi defined legato playing for the first time: "The best general rule is to keep down the keys of the instrument, the FULL LENGTH of every note…" unless they are marked otherwise. It was Clementi who popularized the expressive legato style, which became the preferred keyboard touch of the 19th century.

**Presto.** Sonata-allegro form: Exposition = measures 1–26 (first theme = 1–16; second theme = 16–26); development = 26–44; recapitulation = 44–63 (first theme = 44–52; second theme = 52–63).

The right hand carries the melodic interest throughout this movement, so it should be well-projected at all times. Some pedaling is suggested but the amount indicated by Clementi is usually too much for pianos of today.

**Allegretto moderato.** Form: Binary. Part I = measures 1–49; part II = 50–98; coda = 98–108.

In the first edition this movement was titled "Original Swiss Air." The sixth edition expands this movement by 26 measures as compared to the first edition. A gentle yodeling quality permeates this attractive movement. The dolce markings suggest poco rubato throughout the movement and, as Clementi says, "now and then swelling some notes" (page 8 of his *Introduction*).

**Rondo—Allegro assai.** Rondo form: **A** = measures 1–16; **B** = 16–28; **A**$^1$ = 28–44; bridge = 44–52; coda = 52–58; **C** = 58–74; bridge = 74–84; **D** = 84–96; codetta = 96–103; **A** = 1–16; **B** = 16–28; **A**$^1$ = 28–44; bridge = 44–52; coda = 52–58.

Clementi changed the mood and tempo terms from Allegro di molto in the first edition to Allegro assai here and shortened the movement by 10 measures in the sixth edition as compared with the first edition. This movement is bright and cheerful throughout, even during the *pp* in measures 84–87.

*Waltz in F Major*, Op. 39, No. 4 . . . . . . . . . . . . . . 89

Form: Four parts. Part I = measures 1–16; part II = 17–44 (**A** = 17–32; **B** = 33–44); part III = 45–70 (**A** = 45–52; **B** = 53–70); part I repeated.

This piece comes from Clementi's Op. 39, *Twelve Waltzes for the Pianoforte with Accompaniments for Tambourine and Triangle* published in 1800. The subtitle matches the right-hand melody in measures 1–4. The wedge-shaped staccato marks mean the note receives less time and the staccato sound is more distinct than when dots are used. The right hand frequently crosses over the left hand; keep the right hand close to the left hand when making the crossing.

## CARL DITTERS VON DITTERSDORF (1739–1799)

Dittersdorf, an Austrian composer, was a major figure of the Viennese Classical school. He composed over 40 concertos, chamber music and around 120 symphonies. Most endearing were his comic operas, which combine folklike and *opera buffa* styles.

*Three English Dances*. . . . . . . . . . . . . . . . . . . . . . . 92

**I.** Form: Ternary. Part I = measures 1–8; part II = 8–16; part III = 16–24.

Keep the tempo steady in this humorous dance. Separate eighth and quarter notes while sixteenth notes should be connected. Vary dynamics on repeats.

**II.** Form: Ternary. Part I = measures 1–8; part II = 8–16; part III = 16–24.

Play the small grace notes in measures 17, 19 and 21 on the beat like acciaccaturas (crushed notes). Separate the eighth notes and connect the sixteenths. Vary dynamics on repeats.

**III.** Form: Ternary. Part I = measures 1–8; part II = 9–16; part III = 17–24.

This dance requires a strong opening and closing as well as nicely contrasted dynamics. Keep the eighth notes separated and the sixteenths connected.

## JAN LADISLAV DUSSEK (1760–1812)

Dussek was born in Bohemia, toured widely gaining a brilliant reputation, lived in London for 12 years and died near Paris. His music was praised by Haydn, and Dussek was famous in his own time as pianist and composer. He composed over 40 piano sonatas, around 12 piano concertos and many chamber works (mostly with piano). His early works are Classical in style, as is this polonaise, but after around 1790 his works contain Romantic characteristics anticipating Schubert, Chopin and others.

*Polonaise in F Major*, Op. 16, No. 6 . . . . . . . . . . . 94

Form: Introduction = measures 1–4; **A** = 5–16; **B** = 17–23; **A** = 5–16.

The Polonaise, as originally conceived, was more a stately processional than a dance. The Italian form (*Polacca*) uses a quicker tempo than the Polonaise proper. This polonaise seems to be more *polacca* than polonaise because of its tendency to want to move quickly, possibly because of so many sixteenth notes. Keep the introduction (measures 1–4) and closing strong and stately. Bring out the left-hand parts at measures 15–16 and 21–23.

## ELISABETTA DE GAMBARINI (1731–1765)

De Gambarini was a versatile English composer and orchestral conductor. Also a well-known singer, she sang in the first performance of Handel's *Occasional Oratorio* in 1746. These three dances come from *Six Sets of Lessons for the Harpsichord* composed around 1748.

*Three Dances* . . . . . . . . . . . . . . . . . . . . . . . . . . . . . . 96

**Minuet.** Form: Binary. Part I = measures 1–8; part II = 9–16.

Repeat measures 1–8 *p* after playing them first *f*. Separate quarter notes and connect eighth notes. Chords in measures 8 and 16 could be arpeggiated (from the top downward, which will make the voice leading more clear).

**Tempo di Gavotta.** Form: Binary. Part I = measures 1–12; part II = 13–32 (**A** = 13–24; **B** = 25–32).

This dance is like a two-part invention with one part in each hand. Connect sixteenth notes and separate eighth notes. Vary dynamics on repeats.

**Giga.** Form: Binary. Part I = measures 1–11; part II = 11–24 (**A** = 11–17; **B** = 17–24).

This lively dance will sparkle if you connect eighth notes (unless indicated otherwise) and separate quarter and dotted quarter notes. Vary dynamics on repeats.

## JOHANN WILHELM HÄSSLER (1747–1822)

This German composer's earlier keyboard style shows a preference for the clavichord idiom, but his late works make use of the colors and techniques of the pianoforte. Hässler composed *24 Studies in Waltz Form*, Op. 49 while in Moscow for his students who needed short, easy works and effective practice drills. These 24 short pieces go through all the keys and exhibit classic pianistic figurations. A few contain some unexpected harmonic twists.

*Etude No. 5 in B-flat Major*, Op. 49, No. 5 . . . . . . 100

Form: **A** = measures 1–8; **B** = 8–16; **A**¹ = 16–24.

Flowing sixteenth-note figuration is featured here, first in the left hand (measures 1–3) and then the right hand (measures 4–7). Both hands join in (measures 9–12 and 16–22) and end with strong cadences in measures 7–8 and 23–24.

*Etude No. 6 in B-flat Minor*, Op. 49, No. 6 . . . . . . 101

Form: Binary. Part I = measures 1–16; part II = 16–32.

Left-hand broken octaves are used in part I (measures 1–16) and right-hand broken octaves are heard in part II (measures 16–23) while left-hand broken octaves complete part II (measures 24–30). Long crescendo lines add a dramatic quality (measures 1–4, 9–12, 25–29) to the piece. Repeat No. 5 after No. 6 to produce an **A B A** form.

*Two Scottish Dances* . . . . . . . . . . . . . . . . . . . . . . 102

I. Form: Binary. Part I = measures 1–8; part II = 8–24 (**a** = 8–12; **b**, from part I = 12–16; **a** = 16–20; **b** = 20–24).

Single-note melodies (measures 1–2) are combined with double-note melodies (measures 3–4) to produce a delightful piece; contrasted rhythms also add to the dance character.

II. Form: Binary. Part I = measures 1–8; part II = 8–24.

The opening motif ♪♩. follows a short-long pattern, which is very characteristic of Scottish music. Place a slight emphasis on the thirty-second note. Repeat the first dance for an **A B A** form.

## FRANZ JOSEPH HAYDN (1732–1809)

This great Austrian composer shares with his contemporary Mozart the role of the most famous composers of the 18th century. Haydn greatly shaped the development of the symphony, the string quartet and the sonata. His keyboard works are finally being recognized as a major contribution to the repertoire. Some of his sonatas are masterpieces that cast their shadows into the 19th century and display astonishing formal and stylistic diversity.

*Scherzo in F Major*, Hob. XVI:9 . . . . . . . . . . . . . 104

Form: Binary. Part I = measures 1–8; part II = 8–24 (**a** = 8–16; **b**, from part I = 16–24).

This short bubbly finale is eminently pianistic and fun for audiences and pianists. Keep the left-hand part subdued in measures 9–13 so the right-hand melody may be easily heard. Separate eighth notes and connect sixteenth notes.

*Sonata in E Major*, Hob. XVI:13 . . . . . . . . . . . . . 105

This sonata was possibly completed around 1767; however, researchers have yet to determine the exact date.

**Moderato.** Form: Sonata-allegro. Exposition = measure 1–30; development = 31–53; recapitulation = 54–81; coda = 81–84.

This attractive short movement is full of resonant and expansive contours suggestive of a much larger movement. Decide on a steady pulse for this taut and angular piece. It requires careful articulation as well as rhythmic precision.

**Minuet.** Form: Minuet = measures 1–24; Trio = 25–52; Minuet repeated = 1–24.

Change fingers on the repeated notes to insure clear articulation. Connect eighth notes and separate quarters. In the Trio, keep the right hand close to the keys and play legato.

**Finale—Presto.** Form: Sonata-allegro. Exposition = measures 1–43; development = 43–59; recapitulation = 59–103; coda = 103–107.

This brilliant and jovial Finale projects a strutting rhythm, a kind of pompous or theatrical affectation of dignity. Keep the tempo brisk with a secure two-beat pulse. The parallel thirds (measures 5–7 and similar places) require evenness and finger independence. Crescendo from measure 104 and conclude with a strong "upbeat" ending.

*Sonata in E Minor*, Hob. XVI:34 . . . . . . . . . . . . . 114

This popular sonata dates from around 1783–84.

**Presto.** Sonata-allegro form: Exposition = measures 1–45; development = 46–78; recapitulation = 79–124; coda = 124–127.

Musically captivating and full of uncomplicated patterns, this movement is most accessible in both spirit and texture. Do not set the tempo too fast. A presto in Haydn's day was not as fast as we think of presto today. Take care to connect the double-note legato passages (such as measures 1–4). Make the most of the sectional dynamics in the development section (measures 46–78).

**Adagio.** Sonata-allegro form: Exposition = measures 1–20; development = 21–31; recapitulation = 32–45; coda = 45–49 that leads immediately to the next movement.

The contemplative mood is supported by a highly elaborate melodic line. It must never be rushed and should always sound "at ease" (the literal meaning of adagio). The staccato notes in measures 1, 3, 21, 23 and like passages must be gently separated.

**Vivace molto.** Rondo form: **A** = measures 1–18 (two parts: I = 1–8; II = 8–18); **B** = 18–40 (two parts: I = 18–26; II = 26–40); **A** = 40–58; **C** = 58–68; **A**¹ = 68–76; **B**¹ = 76–100; **A**² = 100–126; coda = 126–136.

This strong driving Finale must be performed in a playful manner (*innocentemente*), but undergirding the movement is an intense character. Select a tempo that lets the pianist always maintain clarity and rhythmic security. Work in a light Alberti bass with a slight emphasis on the first sixteenth note of the group (fifth finger). The final double octave (measure 136) should sound energetic and strong.

## MICHAEL HAYDN (1737–1806)

The Austrian composer, Michael Haydn, was the younger brother of Franz Joseph Haydn. He was a close friend of Mozart. Michael Haydn, Mozart and Anton Cajetan Adlgasser (1729–1777) each composed an act of an oratorio. Michael was very active in church music and composed 38 masses and over 300 other church works. He also wrote around 40 symphonies and much chamber music. Among his students was Carl Maria von Weber.

*Polonaise in C Major* . . . . . . . . . . . . . . . . . . . . . 129

Form: **A** = measures 1–10; **B** = 11–18; **A**¹ 5–10.

Careful attention to articulation is necessary for a fine stylistic performance. Contrasting dynamics add to the attractiveness of the piece.

*Theme with Variations* . . . . . . . . . . . . . . . . . . . 130

Form: Theme and variations.

**Theme.** Be sure the right-hand dotted quarter notes in measures 5–6 are given their full time value.

**Variation I.** On the repeats, bring out the alto-voice (first three beats) in measures 9 and 15.

**Variation II.** Give top voice quarter notes (measures 18 and 24) and alto quarter note (measure 20) their full time value. Also, do not overlook the full value of the left-hand dotted quarter notes in measures 21 and 22.

**Variation III.** This variation features contrasted touches: legato in the right hand and staccato (eighths) and separated quarters in the left hand.

## JAMES HEWITT (1770–1827)

Hewitt was born in Dartmoor, England and followed his father in a brief naval career. Before leaving for America in 1792 he played in an orchestra under Haydn's direction. Hewitt settled first in New York, later in Boston, and was well known as a teacher, conductor, composer, violinist, organist, promoter of city concerts and music publisher. He composed ballad operas, numerous songs and many pieces for the pianoforte, including the famous *Battle of Trenton*, dedicated to George Washington.

*Mark My Alford* . . . . . . . . . . . . . . . . . . . . . . . . . . 132

The song *Mark My Alford* was composed by Samuel Arnold (1740–1802) and used in his opera *Children in the Woods*. Hewitt based this air with variations on the song. It was printed for the first time in 1808 in New York and later issued in Boston and Philadelphia. Mozart used the same tune that is known today as *Twinkle, Twinkle Little Star*.

Form: Theme and variations.

**Theme.** Keep the touch nonlegato.

**Variation I.** Keep both hands legato. The right hand figure may be played like 🎵 .

**Variation II.** Play the short grace note in measure 19 on the beat like a crushed note. Give left-hand down-stem quarter notes in measures 22–23 their full value.

**Variation III.** Keep the left-hand triplet figuration one dynamic level softer than the right hand. In measures 30–31, play the left-hand sixteenth note with the third part of the right-hand triplet.

**Variation IV.** Keep light and pianissimo throughout.

**Variation V.** Shift to a slower tempo and use poco rubato to be sure all the thirty-second notes are clearly heard.

**Variation VI.** In measures 49–50 and 53 play the last eighth-note chord in the right hand with the third part of the left-hand triplet. Also, play the alto-voice eighth notes in measures 54–55 with the third note of the triplet.

**Variation VII.** Bring out the left-hand theme in measures 60–64.

**Variation VIII.** Give all left-hand quarter notes their full value.

**Variations IX and X.** Because of its majestic (Maestoso) quality and strong dynamic level, Variation IX may be more effective played last, following the charming waltz-like Variation X.

## FRANZ ANTON HOFFMEISTER (1754–1812)

This German composer was also a very successful music publisher. By 1785 he had established his firm in Vienna. In 1801 he founded the Bureau de Musique in Leipzig with A. Kühnel. Hoffmeister was a personal friend of Mozart and published several of Mozart's first editions (between K. 478 and 577). C. F. Peters eventually took over the firm. Hoffmeister was a prolific composer and wrote over 66 symphonies, several operas, chamber music, 12 piano sonatas and smaller works and songs.

*Menuettino* . . . . . . . . . . . . . . . . . . . . . . . . . . . . 140

Form: Rondo. **A** = measures 1–8; **B** = 8–22; **A**¹ = 23–30; **C** = 30–42; coda = 42–46.

This "small" minuet includes flowing and varied figuration, and colorful use of acciaccaturas. The *fz*s in measures 4–5 are soft accents because of the *p* at the beginning. Do not rush the right-hand quarter notes in measures 16 and 18–20. The ritardando beginning in measure 44 to the end should be slight.

## JOHANN NEPOMUK HUMMEL (1778–1837)

An Austrian pianist-composer, Hummel lived and studied with Mozart from 1785–87. He also studied with Clementi in London. Hummel toured Europe with great success as a concert pianist. One of the outstanding pianists of his day, he was regarded by some as the equal of Beethoven. His main contribution lies in his solo piano works and piano concertos, which contributed to the development of piano technique.

*Gigue in D Major* . . . . . . . . . . . . . . . . . . . . . . . . 142

Form: Three six-measure periods: I = measures 1–6; II = 7–12; III = 13–18.

This piece is No. 40 in Hummel's *Anweisung zum Piano-forte Spiel* (Method for Piano-forte Playing) printed in Vienna in 1828. This bouncing dance should flow easily by using a fairly light touch.

*Menuet in C Major*, Op. 42, No. 3 . . . . . . . . . . . 143

Form: Ternary. Menuet = measures 1–16; Trio = 16–32; Menuet = 33–52.

The menuet was a slow, stately dance using small, dainty steps in triple time. This menuet (measures 1–16) is contrasted with a second menuet (measures 16–32) called a "Trio," which features the use of more eighth notes. Careful attention to dynamics will add much interest.

## FRIEDRICH KUHLAU (1786–1832)

Kuhlau, a German composer, established himself in Copenhagen after studying in Hamburg. He is best known for his Classical piano works and popular flute music. Kuhlau was the foremost composer of the late-Classical and early-Romantic period in Denmark.

*Six Variations*, Op. 42, No. 1 . . . . . . . . . . . . . . . . 146

Form: Theme and variations.

This cheerful piece was composed in 1822. Following the theme (measures 1–8):

**Variation I** features the melody in the left hand.

**Variation II** highlights the melody in the right hand.

**Variation III** retains the harmony and introduces scalar figuration.

**Variation IV** shifts to the relative minor key (E), using some of the melody, now transposed, and new figuration.

**Variation V** maintains some of the original harmony and features the left-hand part in a rhythmic figure that comes from the opening melody (two sixteenths and an eighth note).

**Variation VI** uses sprightly figuration to end the set in a jovial mood. Be sure the melodic ideas are clearly heard against the accompaniment.

## WOLFGANG AMADEUS MOZART (1756–1791)

Mozart, an Austrian composer, was perhaps the most universal musical genius of all time. His early study was with his father, Leopold. Acclaimed early for his virtuosity on the keyboard, he also mastered violin and organ by the age of seven. His father took him on tour allowing Mozart to meet many of the prominent musicians of his day and become acquainted with a vast amount of music then in vogue. Mozart served as concertmaster in the Archbishop's orchestra in Salzburg until he left for Vienna in 1781. His Vienna years were fruitful but Mozart did not handle money well and he died in need in 1791 while composing a *Requiem* for an unknown nobleman.

Mozart excelled in many musical forms. His style represents a fusion of the national styles of his period, of Italian facility and German craft.

*Adagio in B Minor*, K. 540 . . . . . . . . . . . . . . . . 149

Form: Sonata-allegro. Exposition = measures 1–22; development = 22–35; recapitulation = 36–54; coda = 54–59.

This expressive work was composed on March 19, 1788. It requires a great deal of legato playing. Give full value to the rests in measures 13–14 and 44–45. When playing this piece on a modern piano, the pianist must be careful not to use all the resources of the instrument, or this sensitive masterpiece can easily be ruined by over-pedaling.

*Klavierstück in F Major*, K. 33B . . . . . . . . . . . . . 155

Form: Binary. Part I = measures 1–12; part II = 13–26.

This piece was composed during the end of August and beginning of September 1766. Keep the eighth and quarter notes nonlegato and the sixteenth notes legato. Most of the piece is built around a written-out turn. Vary dynamics on repeats.

*Two Contredanses in G Major*,
    K. 269B, Nos. 1 and 2 . . . . . . . . . . . . . . . . . . 156

These two dances were composed in Salzburg in January 1777 and were written for Johann Rudolf Graf Czernin (1755–?). Czernin was an amateur violinist who played a large part in enlarging amateur music-making in Salzburg.

I. Form: Four Parts. Part I = measures 1–8; part II = 8–16; part III = 16–24; part IV = 24–32.

This dance begins on the upbeat and must sound lighter than the downbeat. Bring out the upper voice in measures 4–6 and 28–30.

II. Form: Four Parts. Part I = measures 1–8; part II = 8–16; part III = 16–24; part IV = 24–32.

The introduction (measures 1–8) is in Andantino tempo, which, in Mozart's day, was a little slower than Andante. The merry contredanse proper begins at measure 8 (Allegro). Keep the touch light in the *p* sections and only a little stronger in the *f* sections.

*Fantasy in D Minor*, K. 397 . . . . . . . . . . . . . . . . . 159

Form: Triparte. Part I (introduction) = measures 1–11; part II = 12–54 (**A** = 12–34; **B** = 35–44; **A**¹ = 45–54); part III = 55–108 (**A** = 55–86; **B** = 87 cadenza; **A**¹ = 88–108).

This work was composed in Vienna in either early 1782 or possibly in 1786–87. It contains three marvelous contrasting sections. After the opening prelude of arpeggios suggesting improvisation, the piece turns to a lyrical and melancholy Adagio section. It then concludes with an upbeat Allegretto section. Mozart left the work unfinished and the final ten measures were added for the Complete Edition published in 1804.

*Sonata in A Minor*, K. 310 . . . . . . . . . . . . . . . . . 166

This great sonata was composed in Paris in 1778. Alfred Einstein describes this work as a "tragic sonata … dramatic and full of unrelieved darkness."[2] It is a superb example of Mozart's "storm and stress" writing. The technical and interpretive demands of this sonata are great.

**Allegro maestoso.** Form: Sonata-allegro. Exposition = measures 1–49 (first subject = 1–16; transition = 16–22; second subject = 22–45; codetta = 45–49); development = 50–79; recapitulation = 80–133 (first subject = 80–97; transition = 97–103; second subject = 103–129; codetta = 129–133).

---

[2] Alfred Einstein, *Mozart* (London: Cassell & Co., Ltd., 1946), 244.

A high intensity level and the dark key of A minor reflect a strong emotional character throughout this movement. The vigorous opening idea with dotted rhythms is supported by continuous repeated chords in the left hand. Quietly moving thirds in measures 5–7 provide contrast. The second subject with many sixteenths provides a cheerful contrast to the opening idea. The development presents the opening idea in the bright relative key of C major but the brightness does not last long. By measure 53 a diminished chord sets the stage to eventually return to the darker key of A minor for the recapitulation. An unrelieved somber quality pervades the complete recapitulation.

Play the grace note in measure 1 short and on the beat. The grace notes in measures 2 and 4 are long, played as eighths. The calando indication in measure 14 requires only a decrescendo to the piano in measure 15. Bring in the left hand very discreetly at measure 33. Begin the trill in measure 39 on the main note, and those in measures 42–43 on the upper note. Play the trills in measures 74–77 as effortlessly as possible. The closing chords in measure 133 are not rolled; they should be full and rich, not percussive.

**Andante cantabile con espressione.** Form: Sonata-allegro. Exposition = measures 1–31 (first subject = 1–14; second subject = 15–29; codetta = 29–31); development = 31–53; recapitulation = 53–86 (first subject = 53–68; second subject = 68–84; codetta = 84–86).

A fine performance of this intimate and deeply felt movement requires an excellent legato and a refined sense of orchestration and articulation. The left hand has a steady quality that supports a more flexible right hand with numerous complex figurations. The opening theme is built on a broken tonic triad: its repetition at measure 5–8 is varied greatly. The second subject features repeated notes, trills and scaler figuration. The development section moves into a dramatic and agitated section (measures 37–53) that finally gives way to the recapitulation.

The grace note in measure 1 should be played expressively before the beat so as not to weaken the dotted rhythm. The thirty-second notes in measure 2 must be absolutely precise. Begin the trill in measure 6 on the main note. Be sure to distinguish between eighth- and sixteenth-note staccatos in measures 15–16. Begin the trill on the upper note in measure 21. The right hand takes over the melody in measure 50 beginning on the second beat.

**Presto.** Form: Sonata-rondo. Exposition = measures 1–142 (first subject = 1–28; second subject 29–87 [based on same material as the first subject]; transition = 87–106; first subject = 107–122; codetta = 122–142); development = 142–175; recapitulation = 175–253 (first subject = 176–203; second subject = 204–246; coda = 246–253).

This dramatic movement, in a free rondo form, uses an insistent micro-motif (dotted quarter and eighth note) that consumes the entire movement. After the somber and breathless character of measures 1–142, a short and calm section in A major (measures 143–175) comes as a complete surprise. The opening idea and mood returns at measure 176 and carries the rest of the movement to a dramatic and propelled-with-octaves (measures 248–253) conclusion.

Measures 21–28 are one long melodic line. Project the imitation of the motif in the bass at measure 248. The quarter rest in measure 253 ends the movement and is part of the performance.

## JOSEF MYSLIVEČEK (1737–1781)

Mysliveček, a Bohemian composer, actively wrote music beginning in 1760. He settled in Italy and presented his first opera in Bergamo in 1765. His operas and oratorios were frequently performed and published during his lifetime. His instrumental music, including symphonies, concertos and chamber music, was also popular. He met Mozart in Bologna in 1770 and from then until 1778 his name was often mentioned in the correspondence of Mozart and his family. His style is often similar to Mozart's and Mozart had only praise for Mysliveček.

***Divertimento No. 6 in C Major*** . . . . . . . . . . . . . . . 190

Form: Rondo. **A** = measures 1–16; **B** = 17–32; **A** = 33–48; **C** = 49–70; **A** = 1–16.

Keep the left-hand Alberti bass legato and at least one dynamic level quieter than the right-hand melody. Be sure the dotted eighth and thirty-second notes in measures 24, 49–50, 55–56 and 58 are played exactly in time so that the thirty-second note does not sound like the third part of a triplet. Give the bass half notes in measures 59–62 and 67–68 their full value to provide finger pedaling.

## CHRISTIAN GOTTLOB NEEFE (1748–1798)

German composer Neefe served as music director of a theater group in 1779 and from around 1780 taught the young Beethoven piano, organ and composition. Neefe composed songs, German stage works and instrumental pieces in the *galant* style, greatly influenced by Mozart. He also wrote an autobiography and essays.

*Toccata in D Minor* . . . . . . . . . . . . . . . . . . . . . . . 193

Form: Sonata-allegro. Exposition = measures 1–30 (theme I = 1–8; theme II = 9–16; theme III = 17–26; codetta = 26–30); development = 31–46; recapitulation = 47–66 (theme I = 48–52; theme II = 53–56; theme III = 57–66); coda = 66–70.

Published in Leipzig in 1774, this brilliant work is the third movement of the second sonata from Neefe's *Six New Sonatas*. Keep the tempo strict with well-articulated figuration. Double-stemmed notes indicate melody, so these should be brought out. Dynamics are original. Project the sudden dynamic changes at measures 5, 11, 14, 20, 22, and other similar places.

## IGNAZ JOSEPH PLEYEL (1757–1831)

An Austrian composer, publisher and piano maker, Pleyel studied and lived with Haydn for five years. He held a number of posts in various parts of Europe and finally settled in Paris in 1795 where he opened a music shop and founded a major publishing house. In 1807, he started a piano factory there. Pleyel's music enjoyed enormous popularity during his lifetime.

*Minuet in C Major* . . . . . . . . . . . . . . . . . . . . . . . 198

Form: Minuet and Trio. Minuet = measures 1–16; Trio = 17–32; Minuet repeated = 1–16.

This piece comes from Pleyel's *Methode de clavier* (1796). Separate quarter notes and connect eighth notes. Most of the melodic activity is assigned to the right hand; be aware of the slight accents in the left hand at measures 21–22. A small ritard. in measure 16 is appropriate when the Minuet is repeated.

*Rondo in G Major* . . . . . . . . . . . . . . . . . . . . . . . 200

Form: Rondo. **A** = measures 1–8; **B** = 8–27; **A** = 27–35; **B** repeated = 8–27; **A** repeated = 27–36; coda = 36–43.

This cheerful piece bounces along in a straightforward manner from beginning to end. A small cadenza may be added at measures 26–27. Vary dynamics on repeats.

## JOHANN FRIEDRICH REICHARDT (1752–1814)

A German composer, Reichardt was also a conductor and writer. He was court composer and conductor to Frederick the Great and Frederick II from 1775–94. He traveled extensively and was acquainted with many important German writers and philosophers. Reichardt was an influential composer of songs and German operettas. He created a wide variety of instrumental music, wrote several books on music and was an important music critic and editor.

*Prelude in C Major* . . . . . . . . . . . . . . . . . . . . . . . 202

Form: Ternary. Part I = measures 1–16; Part II = 16–32; Part I = 1–16.

This piece is excellent for teaching two-note slurs. Be sure to observe them carefully: they appear sometimes in one hand with the second note staccato, or with an overlapping chord in the other hand, as in measure 1. Pay close attention to the contrasting dynamics, which will help convey the *scherzando* (joking) quality of the piece.

## ALEXANDER REINAGLE (1756–1809)

Reinagle, an English-born pianist and composer, taught in Glasgow, Scotland. While touring in Hamburg, Germany, he met C.P.E. Bach (1714–1788), who became a strong admirer of Reinagle's works. Reinagle settled in Philadelphia (1786) where he became an outstanding teacher, theater musician and concert manager. One of his students was Nelly Custis (1779–1852), adopted granddaughter of George Washington (1732–1799). For 15 years he worked in Philadelphia with a theatrical company and composed music for many light stage productions. His four piano sonatas were perhaps the first sonatas written in the USA. He was the most outstanding of late 18th-century American composers. He is buried in Baltimore.

*Steer Her Up and Had Her Gawn* . . . . . . . . . . . . 203

Form: Theme and four variations.

A Scottish tune with variations, this piece was published in a collection in Philadelphia in 1787. Scottish tunes frequently contained unusual and wayward modulations, and because Reinagle had lived in Scotland, he knew how to handle them. Part of the Scottish flavor in tunes results from the fourth and seventh scale degrees sometimes being omitted. An unusual modulation occurs in measures 11–12, 27–28, 43–44, 59–60 and 75–76: it is called a sidestep, an immediate modulation moving up or down a whole step. Keep the touch light and the tempo brisk.

## FERDINAND RIES (1784–1838)

A German pianist and composer, Ries studied piano with Beethoven from 1802 to 1804. He often acted as Beethoven's secretary and copyist. After spending some time in Paris, he moved to London (1813–24) where his works were often heard at the Philharmonic Society concerts. He represented Beethoven in dealings with London publishers. His compositions owe much to Beethoven's style.

*Trifle*, Op. 58, No. 12 . . . . . . . . . . . . . . . . . . . . . . 207

Form: Rondo. **A** = measures 1–16 (part I = 1–8; part II = 8–16); **B** = 16–32 (part I = 16–24; part II = 24–32); **A** = 1–16; **C** = 32–56 (part I = 32–40; part II = 40–56); **A** = 1–16.

This piece comes from a set of *Twelve Trifles*, composed in 1815. Beethoven's bagatelles strongly influenced these pieces. No. 12 almost seems like a model for some of Schubert's *Moments musicaux*. It should flow easily and gracefully: measures 1–16, 32–39, and 48–56 have the character of a *ländler* (a slow waltz). Pay careful attention to the articulation in measures 2, 4, 6 and 14 with their slurs, staccatos and tenutos. Trio I should move along slightly faster than the first section (measures 1–16). Trio II should return to the opening tempo (measure 1), until measures 40 (beat 3) through 48: these eight measures should move along a little faster than measures 32–40 (first two beats). The pickup to measures 49–56 should return to the opening tempo (measure 1).

## FRANZ SCHUBERT (1797–1828)

Schubert was born and died in Vienna, Austria. He was one of the greatest songwriters the world has ever known, but he also composed chamber music, symphonies, operas and music for the piano. In the works of his last eight years he achieved a new synthesis using his individualized melodic gifts, his Romantic feeling for sonority and traditional forms.

*Five Écossaises* . . . . . . . . . . . . . . . . . . . . . . . . . . . . 210

For a discussion of *Écossaises* see Beethoven, *Six Écossaises*, WoO 83, page 9.

**I.** (A-flat major, D. 299, No. 1). Form: Binary. Part I = measures 1–9; part II = 10–17.

Use legato and staccato touches to create strong contrasts. Repeat both sections varying the dynamics.

**II.** (B minor, D. 977, No. 7). Form: Two eight-measure phrases (plus the first and second endings). Phrase 1 = measures 1–10; phrase 2 = 11–19.

Although this dance is written in a minor key, it has a cheerful quality. Play the unslurred quarter and eighth notes nonlegato. Since the piece is so short, the editor recommends varying the dynamics during the repeat.

**III.** (G major, D. 735, No. 1). Form: Binary. Part I = measures 1–4; part II = measures 5–8.

This little dance begins and ends strongly with quieter material in between. Play the left hand staccato and the right hand legato at measures 3–6.

**IV.** (E minor, D. 735, No. 2). Form: Binary. Part I = measures 1–4; part II = 5–8.

Keep the accents light in measures 1–4. Repeat both parts and on the repeat, bring out the left-hand part in measures 5–6.

**V.** (B minor, D. 783, No. 1). Form: Binary. Part I = measures 1–8 repeated; part II = 9–24 (**A** = 9–16; **B** = 17–24).

Keep the left-hand eighths in measures 1–8 and 17–23 nonlegato. Bring out the tenor voice in measures 13–16.

*Two Ländler,* D. 366, Nos. 3 and 4 . . . . . . . . . . . 213

The ländler is a type of slow waltz. A little slower than the waltz, it should be well accented and played in a moderate tempo with a swaying motion.

**I.** (No. 3 in A minor). Form: Binary. Part I = measures 1–8; part II = 8–16.

Keep the touch legato throughout this very expressive piece. Vary dynamics on repeats.

II. (No. 4 in A minor). Form: Binary. Part I = measures 1–8; part II = 8–16.

Pay close attention to the right-hand two-note slurs in measures 6–7 and 9–15. Vary dynamics on repeats.

### *German Dance in C Major*, D. 41, No. 20 . . . . . . 214

Form: Ternary. **A** = measures 1–16; **B** = 16–32; **A** = 1–16.

The German Dance was a lively dance popular in Austria and South Germany between the 18th and early 19th centuries. This was a dance for couples in fast triple meter. The term *German Dance* was eventually superseded by the term *waltz*. A fairly strict tempo should be maintained throughout the dance. The tempo at the end of the piece should be approximately the same as that of the beginning.

### *Hungarian Melody*, D. 817 . . . . . . . . . . . . . . . . . 216

Form: Triparte. Part I = measures 1–24; part II = 25–48 (**A** = 25–37; **B** = 37–48); part I in subdominant = 49–72; closing = 73–103 using material from part II (74–86); coda = 89–103.

This piece was composed on September 2, 1824 while Schubert was staying in Zseliz, Hungary, where he was teaching piano to the daughters of Count Johann von Esterházy (1775–1834). The melody may have been one that Schubert heard sung in the Esterházy kitchen. He used it again in the *Divertissement à la Hongroise* for piano duet. The *Hungarian Melody* has similarities to the F minor *Moments musicaux*, Op. 94, No. 3. The right hand always has the melody, which should be well projected over the left-hand accompaniment.

### *Impromptu in A-flat Major*, Op. 142, No. 2; D. 935 . . . . . . . . . . . . . . . . . . . . . . . . . . . . . 220

Form: Ternary. Allegretto = measures 1–46; Trio = 46–98; Allegretto = 98–144; coda = 144–148.

This piece is from a set of *Four Impromptus* that Schubert composed in 1827. In general the tempo should be strictly retained throughout, but the editor suggests an increase in tempo in measures 65–68 and a broadening in measures 75–78. A broad ritard.

in measures 96–98 is necessary to prepare for the recapitulation of the Allegretto.

### *March in B Minor* (no Deutsch number). . . . . . . . 226

Form: Ternary. March = measures 1–35; Trio = 36–64; March = 1–35.

This piece was written on August 15, 1822 and dedicated to Ferdinand Piranger (1780–1829), a Viennese court official. In the Trio, play the left-hand eighth notes nonlegato and the right-hand melody legato.

### *Moments musicaux*, Op. 94, Nos. 3 and 6; D. 780 . . 229

Schubert published the Op. 94 set of six *Moments musicaux* in 1828, but No. 3 was published in December 1823 with the title *Air Russe*. The title was probably Schubert's as was the title of No. 6, *Plaintes d'un Troubador*, first published in December 1824.

**No. 3 in F Minor.** Form: Rondo. Introduction = measures 1–2, **A** = 3–10; **B** = 11–26; **A** = 27–34; **C** = 35–44; coda = 45–54.

This is probably Schubert's best known piano piece. A pianissimo staccato and careful balance of hands is required. Avoid abrupt tempo changes. All appoggiaturas are short, unaccented and sound better if played slightly before the beat.

**No. 6 in A-flat Major.** Form: Ternary. **A** = measures 1–77 (part I = 1–16; part II = 16–28; part III = 28–39; part IV = 39–53; part I<sup>a</sup> = 53–77); **B** = 77–115; **A** = 1–77.

An elegant legato touch is required for most of this piece. Bring out the melody in the top voice throughout. During the repeats some of the inner moving lines should be brought out as in measures 16–19, 24–28, 40–42 and similar places. Play all appoggiaturas short and unaccented, slightly before the beat.

## RAYNOR TAYLOR (1747–1825)

Born in England, Taylor was educated in the King's Singing School at the Chapel Royal. As a young man, he was director of the famous Saddler's Wells Theater in London. In 1792, he arrived in Baltimore and for a few months was organist at St. Anne's Church in Annapolis. After a few months he moved to Philadelphia where he was active as a singer, teacher and organist of St. Peter's Church. Taylor contributed to the arts in late 18th- and early 19th-century America.

## Rondo in G Major . . . . . . . . . . . . . . . . . . . . . . . . 234

Form: Rondo. **A** = measures 1–8; **B** = 8–16; **A** = 16–24; **C** = 24–36; **A** = 36–44; **D** = 44–52; **E** = 52–64; bridge with cadenza = 64–72; **A**¹ = 72–80; **F** = 80–87; coda = 88–95.

This piece was published in Philadelphia as early as 1794. The graceful rondo theme uses imitation, a technique rarely used in American works of the period. Notice that the left hand leads at the pickup to measure 73, the reverse of the opening of the piece.

## DANIEL GOTTLOB TÜRK (1750–1813)

Türk, a German, devoted himself to music education for the young and became the foremost piano teacher of his time. His *School of Piano Playing* (1789) was used by many piano teachers during his life. Beethoven used it and Robert Schumann was greatly influenced by it. Türk composed 48 sonatas and many shorter pieces for the keyboard.

## Sonatina in F Major . . . . . . . . . . . . . . . . . . . . . 238

This piece was composed in 1785.

**Allegro, ma non tanto.** Form: Sonatina. Exposition = measures 1–16; development = 17–24; recapitulation = 25–36.

This cheerful movement must not go too fast but should be played at a brisk moderato. Incorporate the ornaments into the melodic line and make them sound as smooth as possible. Separate quarter notes and connect eighth notes.

**Larghetto con tenerezza.** Form: Sonatina. Exposition = measures 1–8; development = 8–16; recapitulation = 16–24.

This movement must move slowly so that the tender (*tenerezza*) quality can be brought out. Work out the ornaments carefully so that they can strengthen the expression of the passions and feelings of the movement. The *pf* signs in measures 2, 6, 12, 18 and 22 mean *poco forte* or somewhat loudly.

**Poco allegro.** Form: Rondo. **A** = measures 1–8; **B** = 9–12; **A**¹ = 13–20; coda = 21–26.

Türk defines allegro as "swiftly," so this movement should move "a little swiftly." Changing fingers on repeated notes should aid in producing a clear articulation. Vary dynamics on repeats.

## CARL MARIA VON WEBER (1786–1826)

A German composer, Weber studied in Salzburg with Michael Haydn (1737–1806) and in Vienna with Abbé Vogler (1749–1814). He was dedicated to a new kind of opera uniting all the arts and, above all, his wish to communicate feeling. He served as director of the opera in Prague from 1812–16. His own operatic success in Dresden (1817), Berlin (1821), Vienna (1823), and London (1826) support his fame as the founder of the German Romantic School. His melodic and harmonic style is rooted in Classical principles, but as he matured he experimented with chromaticism. Weber was also active as a critic, virtuoso pianist and chapel master.

## Three Écossaises . . . . . . . . . . . . . . . . . . . . . . . . . . 241

For a discussion of *Écossaises* see Beethoven, *Six Écossaises*, **WoO** 83, page 9. These three *écossaises* may be played **individually** or as a group.

**I.** (D major, no opus number). Form: Binary. Part I = measures 1–8; part II = 8–16.

This dance was composed in the summer of 1802 when Weber was 16. Contrast strongly the required legato and staccato touches. Vary dynamics on repeats.

**II.** (D major, Op. 4, No. 5). Form: Ternary. **A** = measures 1–16; **B** (Trio) = 17–32; **A** = 1–16.

The Op. 4 dances date from 1801. Take all repeats and vary dynamics on the repeats.

**III.** (D minor, Op. 4, No. 6). Form: Ternary. **A** = measures 1–16; **B** (Trio) = 17–32; **A** = 1–16.

Aim for strongly accented chords in measures 1, 2, 5 and 6. In the Trio, be sure all dotted half notes are held for their full time value.

## SAMUEL WESLEY (1766–1837)

Wesley was born in Bristol, England and died in London. He was the son of Charles Wesley and nephew of John Wesley, the founders of Methodism. Samuel began to compose when he was eight years old. He was one of the earliest English Bach enthusiasts and played an important part in the Bach revival. He was regarded as the greatest organist of his day, but his career was interrupted by recurring illness stemming from an injury in 1787. Even so, he continued concertizing until the year of his death. He composed orchestral music, songs and piano music as well as much church music.

*Prelude in A Major* . . . . . . . . . . . . . . . . . . . . . . . 244

Form: Binary. Part I = measures 1–10 repeated; part II = 10–30.

The hands have contrasting touches (legato and staccato) playing at the same time (measures 1–2, 5–9, 11–13 and similar places) making it a good piece for developing independence of hands. Sixteenth notes are played legato.

*Sonata in B-flat Major*, Op. 5, No. 2 . . . . . . . . . . . 246

This work is from *Four Sonatas and Two Duets for the Piano Forte*, dated 1793.

**Hornpipe.** Form: Ternary. **A** = measures 1–8; **B** = 9–20; **A** = 1–8.

The ♪. ♪ figure may be played ♪.. ♪ throughout this movement. Keep the left-hand quarter notes nonlegato unless indicated otherwise. Vary dynamics on repeats. Use plenty of rhythmic drive.

**Waltz.** Form: Rondo. **A** = measures 1–8; **B** = 9–16; **A** = 17–24; **C** = 25–32; **A** = 33–40; **D** = 41–56; **A** = 57–64; **E** = 65–80.

Give the left-hand dotted quarter notes (as in measures 1–6) their full value to serve as finger pedaling. Play the sixteenth notes legato.

# Sonata in F Major

Rafael Anglés
(ca. 1730–1816)

(a) Dynamics are editorial.

(b)

# Bagatelle in D Major

Ludwig van Beethoven (1770–1827)
Op. 119, No. 3

(a) Pedal indications are Beethoven's except those in parentheses in measure 8.

D.C. al Coda

Coda

# Bagatelle in C Major

Ludwig van Beethoven (1770–1827)
Op. 119, No. 8

**Moderato cantabile**

(a) Pedal indications are Beethoven's.

# Bagatelle in F Major

Ludwig van Beethoven (1770–1827)
Op. 33, No. 3

30

# Bagatelle in G Major

Ludwig van Beethoven (1770–1827)
Op. 126, No. 1

**Andante con moto**
*Cantabile e compiacevole*
(In a singing and pleasing style)

# 33

*La seconda parte due volte*
(Play the second part twice)

ⓒ Fingerings in measure 36 are Beethoven's.

# Country Dance in C Major

Ludwig van Beethoven (1770–1827)
WoO 14, No. 1

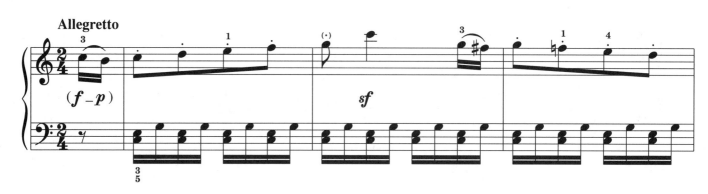

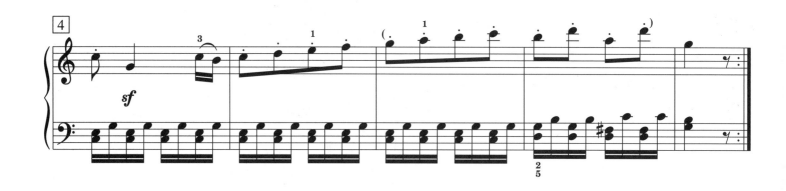

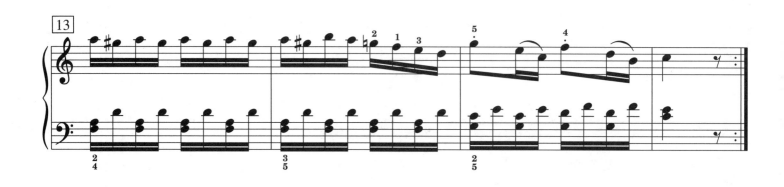

# Country Dance in E-flat Major

Ludwig van Beethoven (1770–1827)
WoO 14, No. 7

# Für Elise

Ludwig van Beethoven (1770–1827)
WoO 59

Poco moto

(a) Pedal indications are Beethoven's in measures 2–4, 10–14 and 79–83. All others in parentheses are editorial.

(d) Beethoven's pedal indications in measures 79–83 cause too much blur on today's pianos. The editor suggests flutter pedal through measures 82–83.

# Six Easy Variations on an Original Theme

Ludwig van Beethoven (1770–1827)
WoO 77

**Theme**

## Variation I

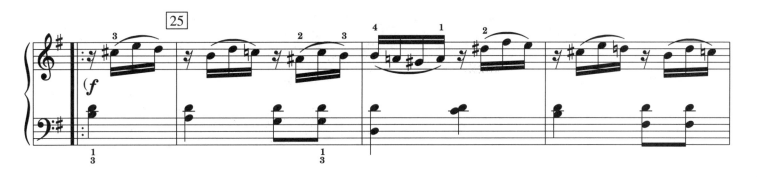

## Variation II

## Variation III

## Variation IV

**Poco sostenuto**

## Variation V

46

## Variation VI

# Six Écossaises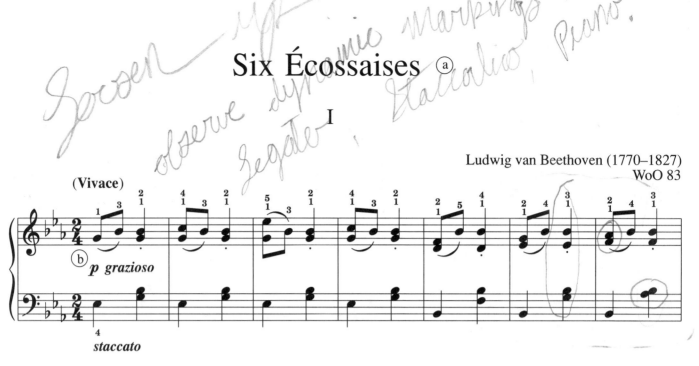

## I

Ludwig van Beethoven (1770–1827)
WoO 83

*attacca*

(a) Thematic unity requires these six *écossaises* to be played as a group.

(b) Articulation is editorial.

# II

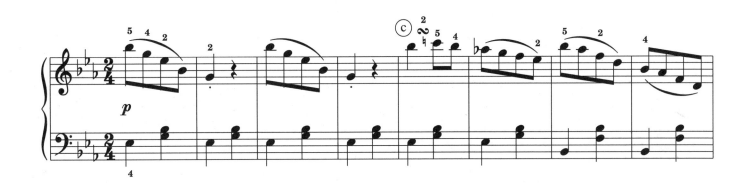

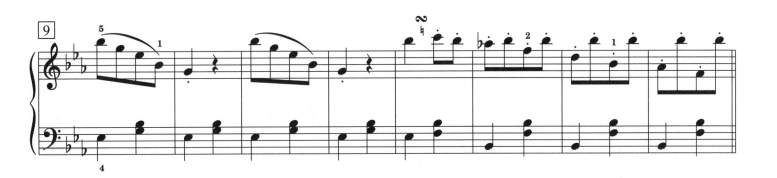

*attacca*

# III

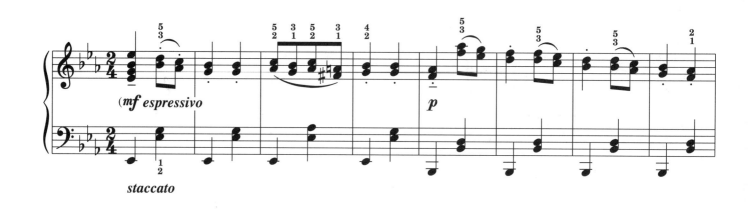

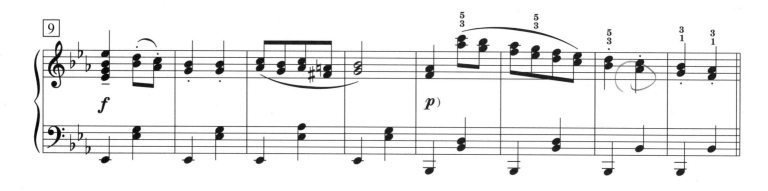

*attacca*

# IV

*attacca*

# V

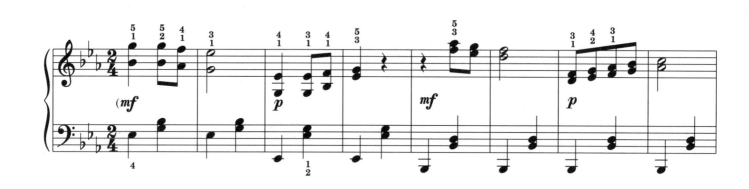

*attacca*

## VI

# Sonata in G Minor
## ("Easy Sonata")

Ludwig van Beethoven (1770–1827)
Op. 49, No. 1

(a) "Easy Sonata" is Beethoven's own title.

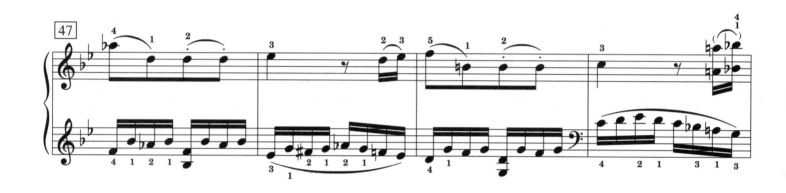

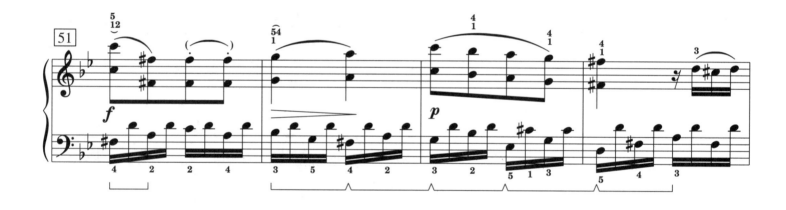

(e)  Play the grace note slightly before the beat.

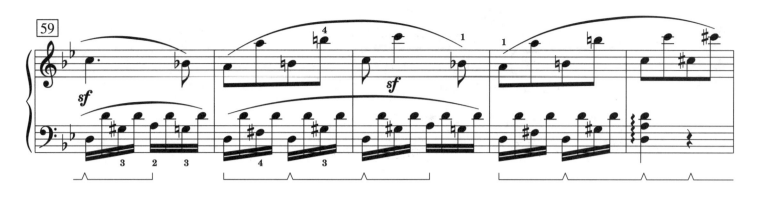

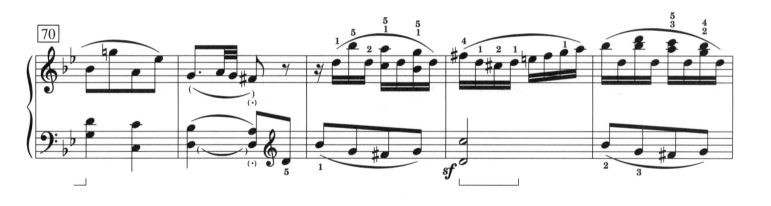

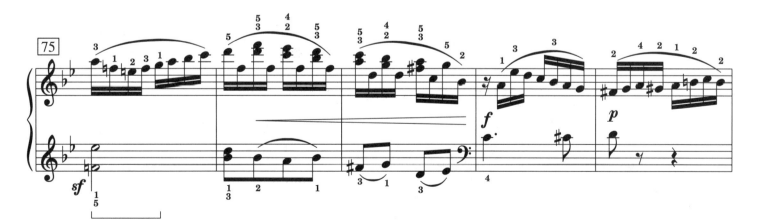

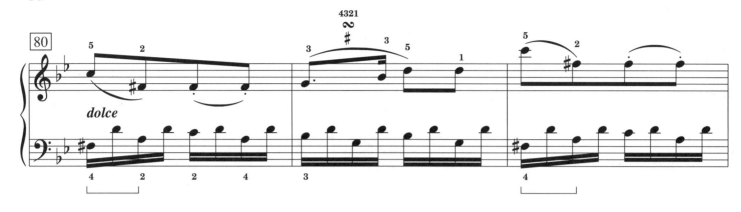

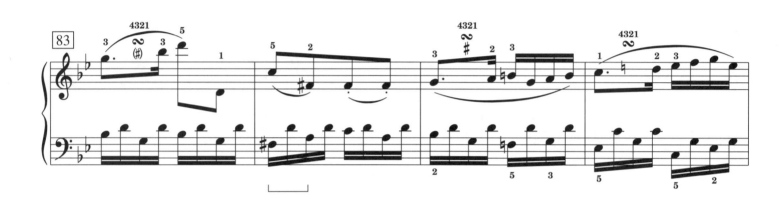

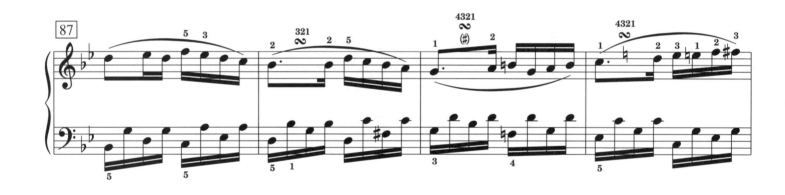

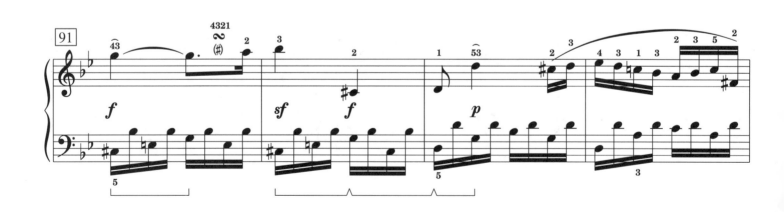

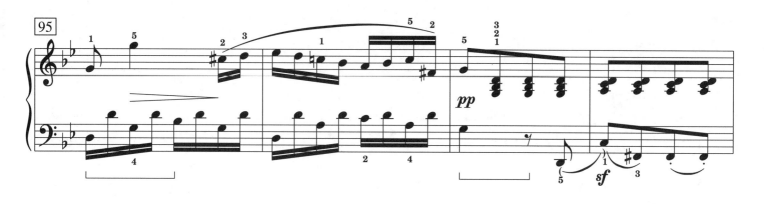

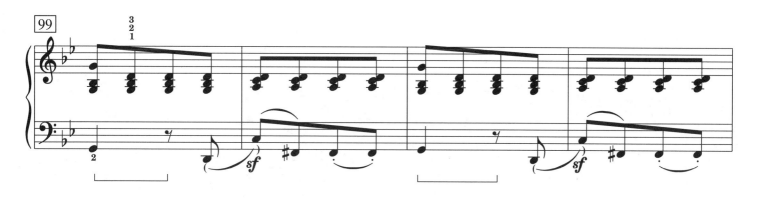

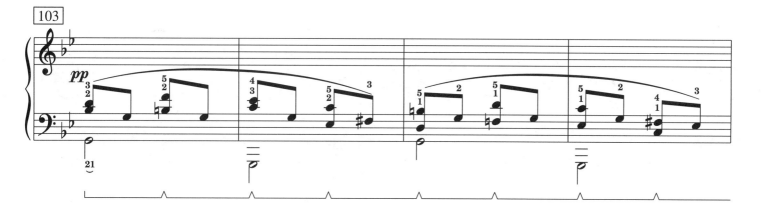

60

# Rondo

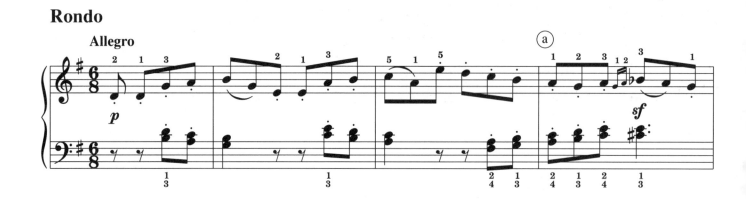

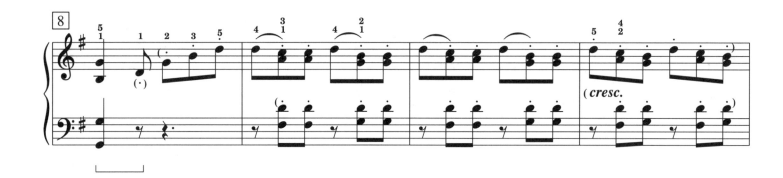

62

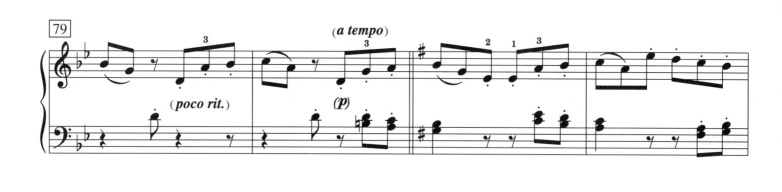

# Sonatina in D Major

Georg Anton Benda
(1722–1795)

ⓐ Dynamics and articulation are editorial.

d This turn is recommended in place of the trill.

# Sonata in B-flat Major

Domenico Cimarosa
(1749–1801)

(a) Dynamics and articulation are editorial.

(b) Play the RH grace notes as triplets with the fourth sixteenth note of the LH group.

73

# Preludio alla Haydn

Muzio Clementi (1752–1832)
Op. 19, No. 2

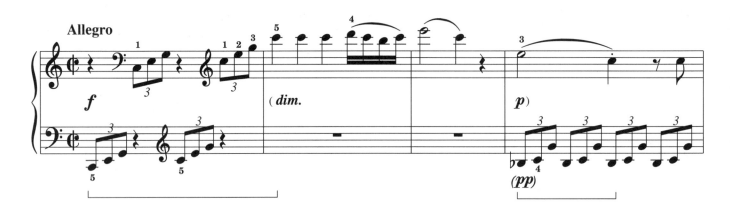

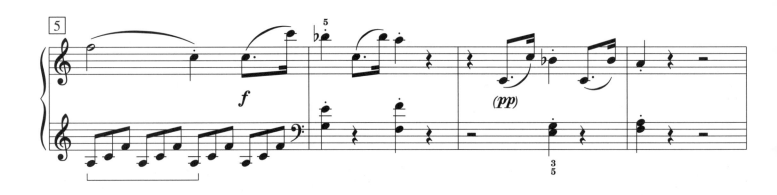

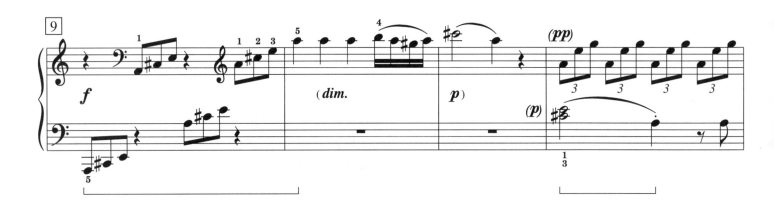

a  Play the grace note slightly before the beat.

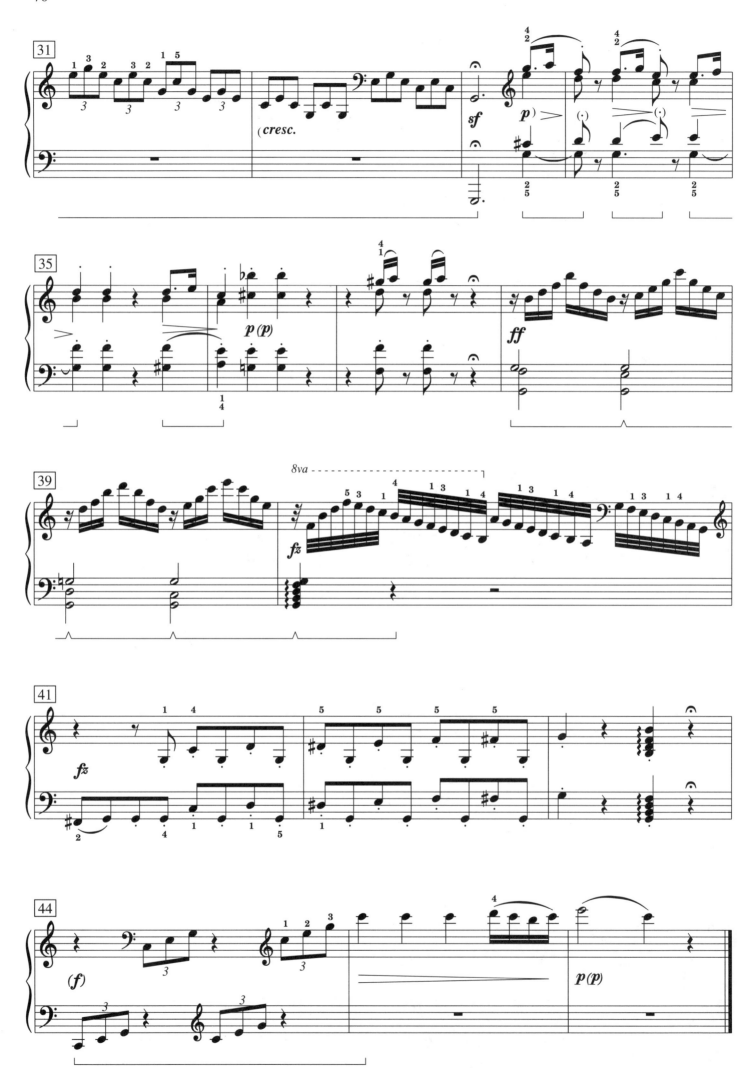

# Sonatina in G Major

Muzio Clementi (1752–1832)
Op. 36, No. 5

(a) 

(b) Fingerings are Clementi's.

(c) Clementi indicated pedal from the beginning of measure 9 to the first beat of measure 11.

(d) Clementi indicated pedal to be held through all of measure 12, changed, and held down through all of measure 13.

Clementi indicated pedal from the beginning of measure 31 to the second beat of measure 32.

f  Clementi indicated pedal from the beginning of measure 45 to the first beat of measure 47.

g  Clementi indicated pedal from the fourth beat of measure 48 to the first beat of measure 50.

**Allegretto moderato**

(b) The early edition contains no pedal for this movement. In the Sixth Edition, Clementi indicated pedal: measure 13 to first beat of 18; measure 20 to second beat of 25; measure 33 to first beat of 37; measure 57 to second beat of 62; measure 70 to first beat of 74; measure 75 to second beat of 76; measure 86 to second beat of 88; measure 92 to second beat of 94.

# Rondo

**Allegro assai**

(a)    Clementi indicated pedal from the first beat of measure 26 to the second beat of measure 29.

(b)    Clementi indicated pedal from the first beat of measure 100 to the end of measure 103.

*D.C. al Fine*

# Waltz in F Major

Muzio Clementi (1752–1832)
Op. 39, No. 4

**Allegro ben marcato**

ⓐ   Fingerings are editorial.

90

D.C. al Fine

# Three English Dances

Carl Ditters von Dittersdorf
(1739–1799)

(a) Dynamics are editorial in all three dances.

## II

III

# Polonaise in F Major

Jan Ladislav Dussek (1760–1812)
Op. 16, No. 6

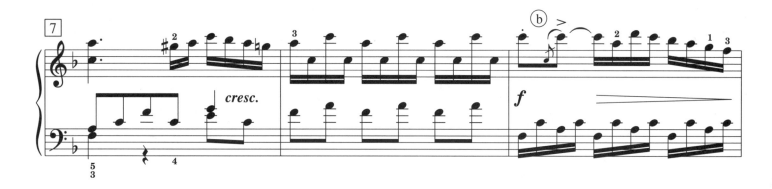

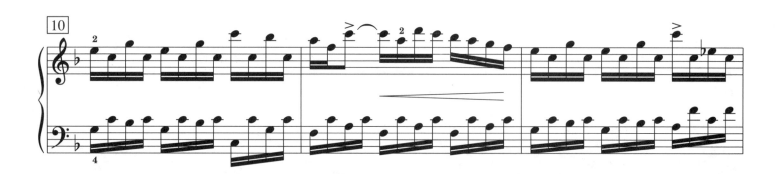

(a) Dynamic and articulation marks are editorial.

(b) Play the grace notes in measures 9, 13 and 14 slightly before the beat.

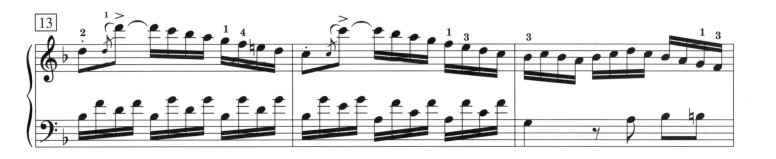

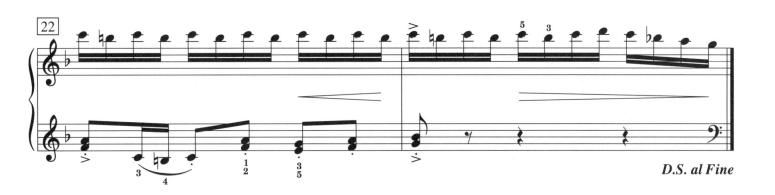

D.S. al Fine

# Three Dances

## Minuet

Elisabetta de Gambarini
(1731–1765)

**(Moderato)**

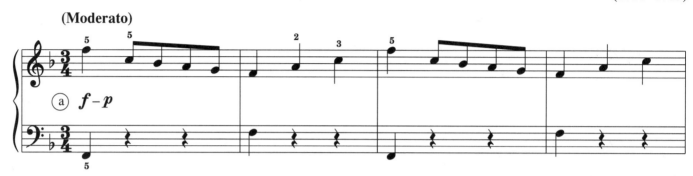

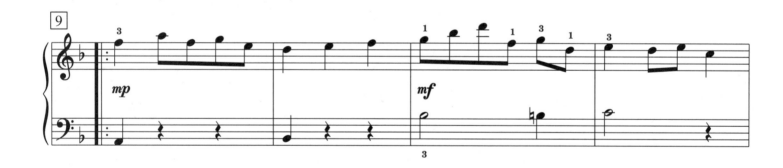

ⓐ  Dynamics are editorial.

ⓑ

# Tempo di Gavotta

(a) Dynamics are editorial.

98

# Giga

(a)  Dynamics and articulation are editorial.

# Etude No. 5 in B-flat Major

Johann Wilhelm Hässler (1747–1822)
Op. 49, No. 5

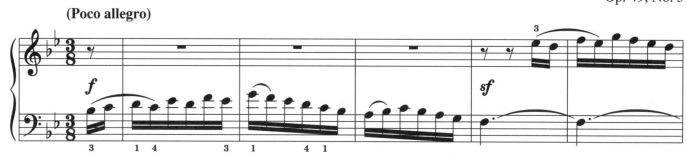

(a) Play the grace note slightly before the beat.

# Etude No. 6 in B-flat Minor

Johann Wilhelm Hässler (1747–1822)
Op. 49, No. 6

*D.C. No. 5 al Fine*

# Two Scottish Dances

I

Johann Wilhelm Hässler
(1747–1822)

(a) Dynamics and articulation are editorial in both dances.

# II

**(Allegretto scherzando)**

# Scherzo in F Major

Franz Joseph Haydn (1732–1809)
Hob. XVI:9

(a) Dynamics are editorial.

# Sonata in E Major

Franz Joseph Haydn (1732–1809)
Hob. XVI:13

ⓐ Dynamics are editorial throughout the sonata.

106

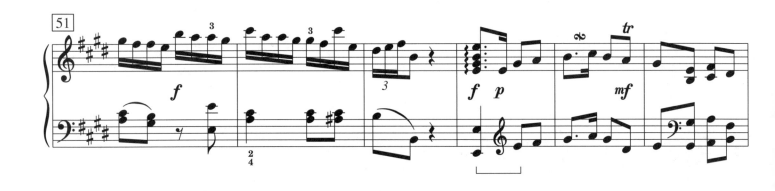

# Minuet

(c) In the case of an appoggiatura followed by a rest, the resolving note is sounded in place of the rest.

**Trio**

*Minuet da Capo*

## Finale

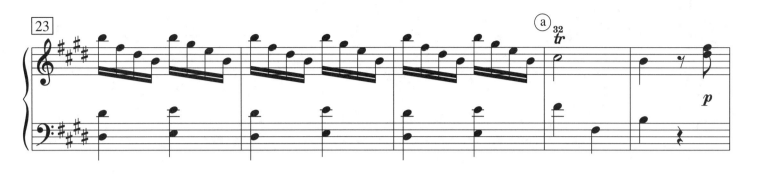

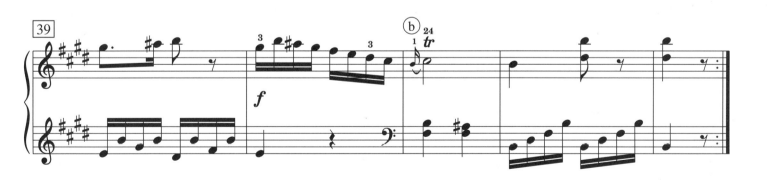

# Sonata in E Minor

Franz Joseph Haydn (1732–1809)
Hob. XVI:34

attacca subito

122

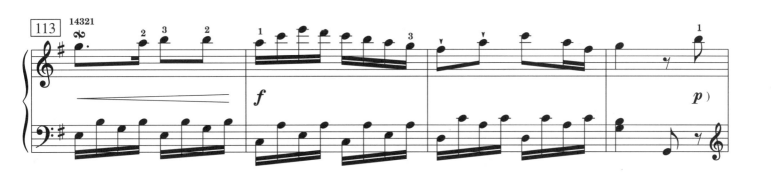

# Polonaise in C Major

Michael Haydn
(1737–1806)

(a) Dynamics and articulation are editorial.

# Theme with Variations

Michael Haydn
(1737–1806)

**Theme**
(Moderato)

**Variation I**

ⓐ Dynamics and articulation are editorial.

## Variation II

## Variation III

(b)  Suggested variation on repeat:

# Mark My Alford

James Hewitt
(1770–1827)

(a) Dynamics and articulation are editorial.

## Variation III

**D.C. (Variation II) al Fine**

**D.C. (Variation III) al Fine**

ⓓ  Play the grace note on the beat like a crushed note.

## Variation IV

(Allegro)

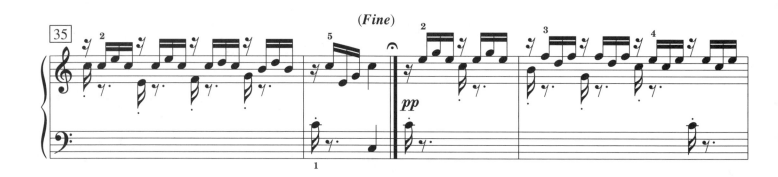

*D.C. (Variation IV) al Fine*

## Variation V

Adagio (cantabile)

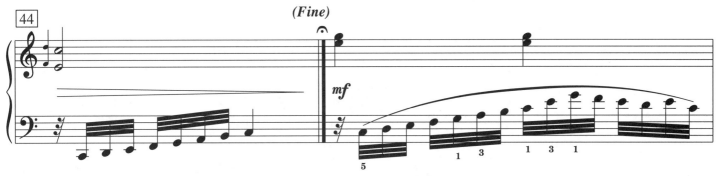

*D.C. (Variation V) al Fine*

## Variation VI

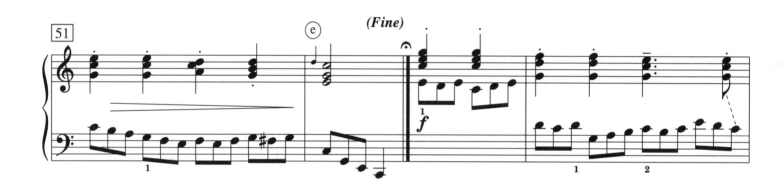

*D.C. (Variation VI) al Fine*

## Variation VII

**Lento (con espressivo)**

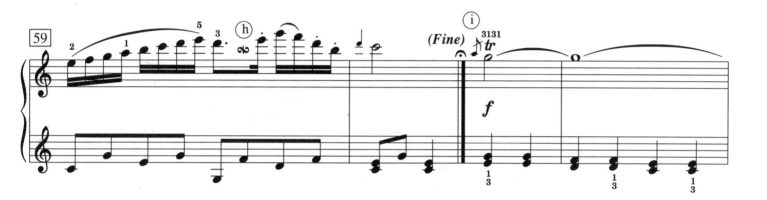

*D.C. (Variation VII) al Fine*

## Variation VIII

## Variation IX

(Maestoso)

*sempre staccato*

*D.C. (Variation IX) al Fine*

## Variation X

# Menuettino

Franz Anton Hoffmeister
(1754–1812)

(a) Articulation is editorial.

(b) Play the grace note on the beat like a crushed note.

# Gigue in D Major

Johann Nepomuk Hummel
(1778–1837)

ⓐ Play the grace note on the beat like a crushed note.

# Menuet in C Major

Johann Nepomuk Hummel (1778–1837)
Op. 42, No. 3

**Tempo di Menuetto**

(a) Dynamics and articulation are editorial.

(b)

(c)

**Trio**

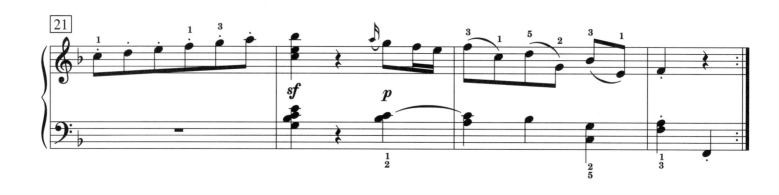

(d)   Play the grace note on the beat like a crushed note.

(e)

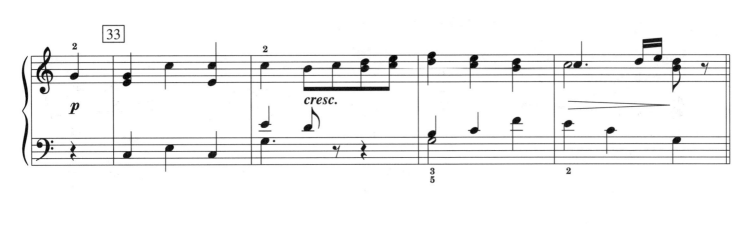

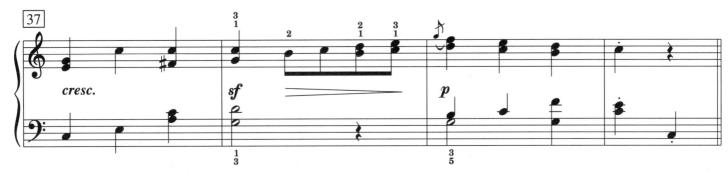

# Six Variations

**Theme**

Friedrich Kuhlau (1786–1832)
Op. 42, No. 1

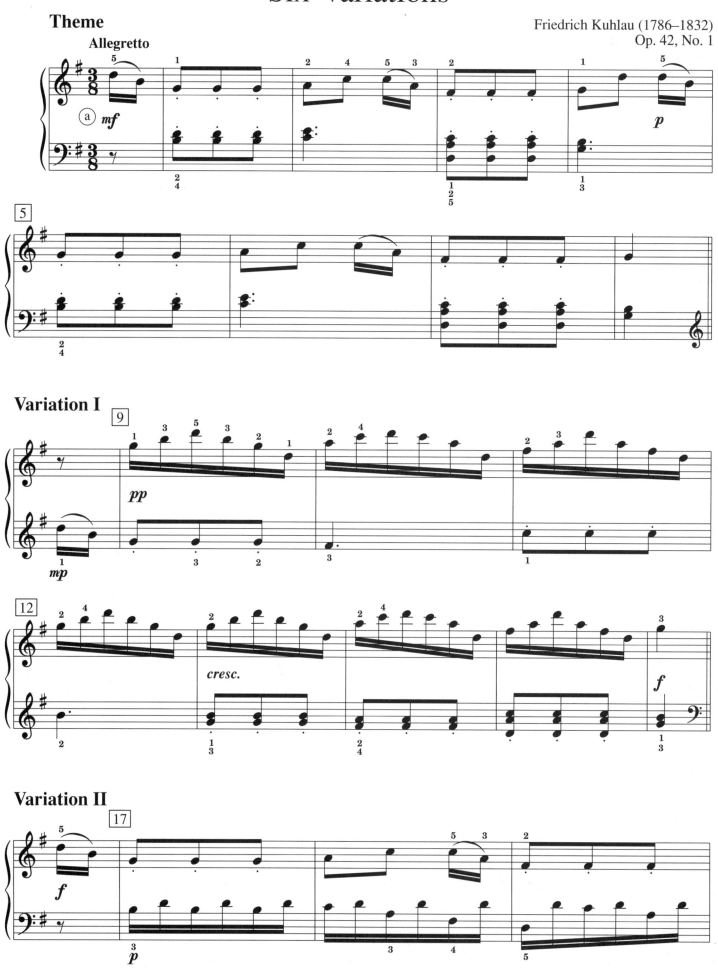

**Variation I**

**Variation II**

ⓐ Dynamics and articulation are editorial.

## Variation III

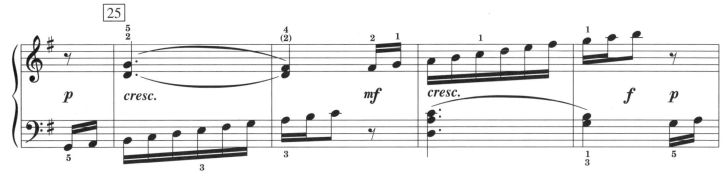

## Variation IV

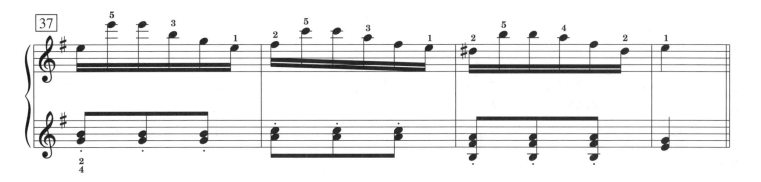

148

## Variation V

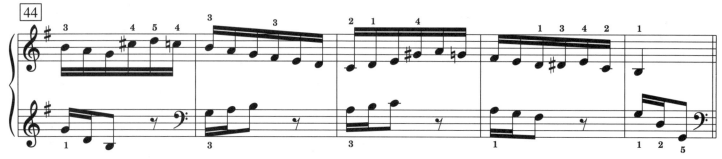

## Variation VI

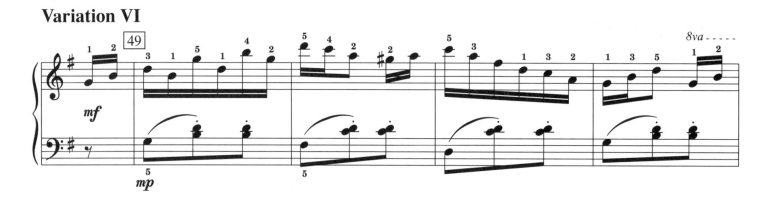

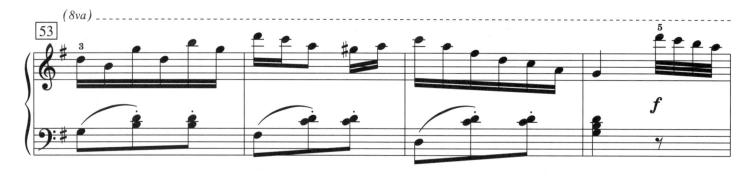

# Adagio in B Minor

Wolfgang Amadeus Mozart (1756–1791)
K. 540

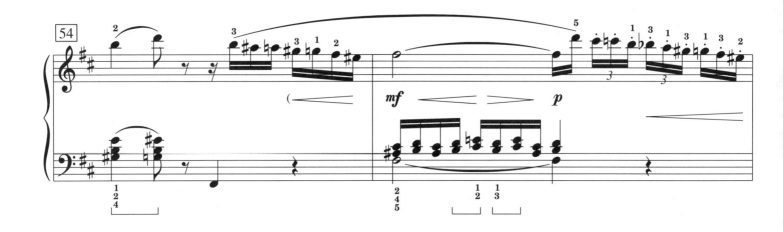

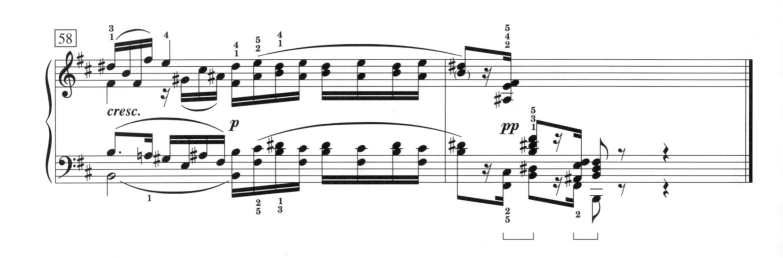

# Klavierstück in F Major

Wolfgang Amadeus Mozart (1756–1791)
K. 33B

(a) Dynamics are editorial.

# Two Contredanses in G Major

## I

Wolfgang Amadeus Mozart (1756–1791)
K. 269B, Nos. 1 and 2

II

Andantino

# Fantasy in D Minor

Wolfgang Amadeus Mozart (1756–1791)
K. 397

(a) The omission of this tie in the original edition was probably an engraver's error.

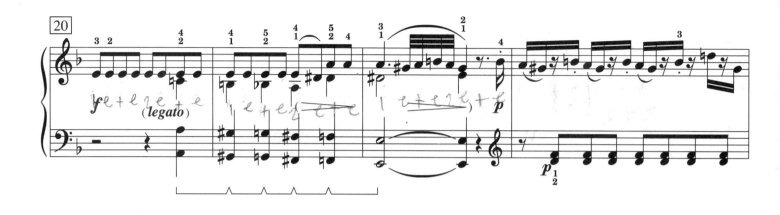

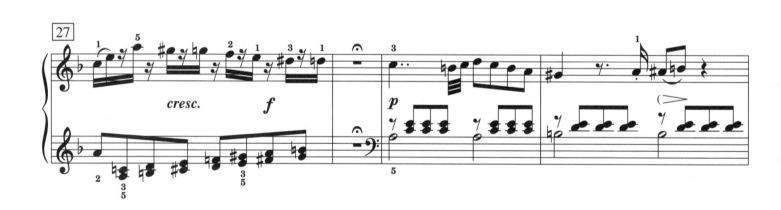

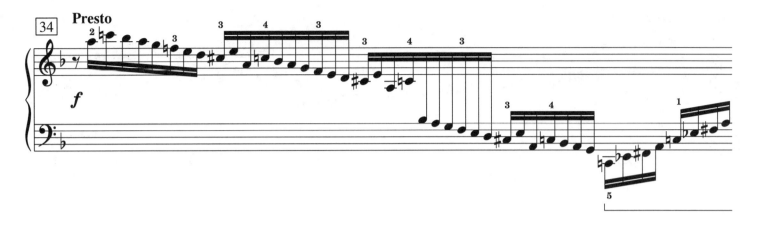

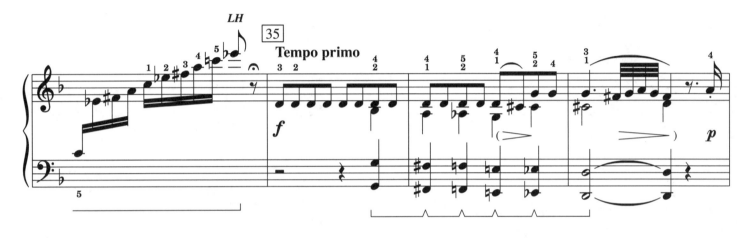

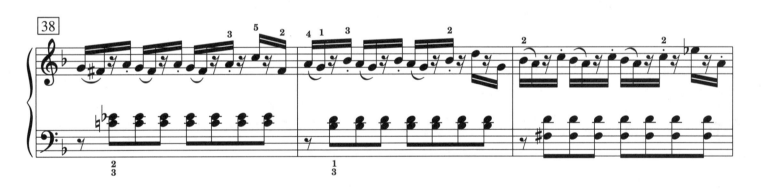

162

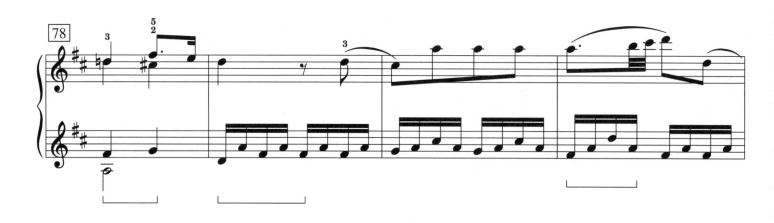

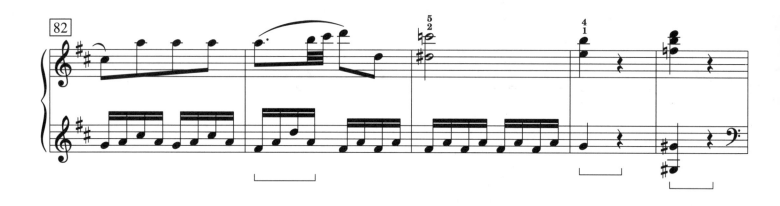

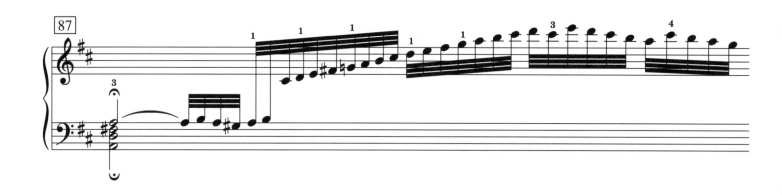

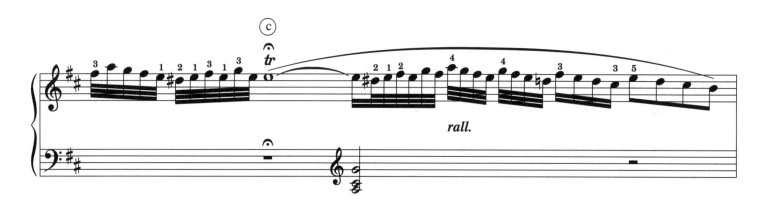

ⓒ  Begin trill on E.

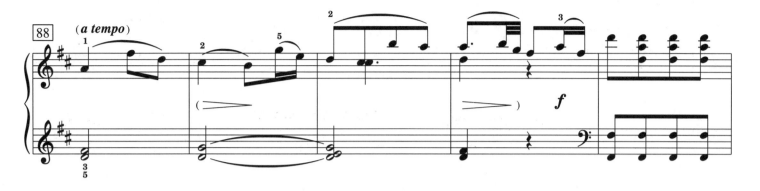

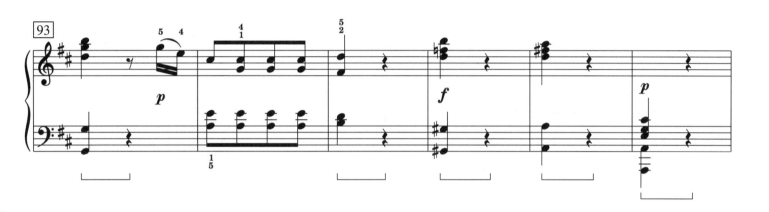

# Sonata in A Minor

Wolfgang Amadeus Mozart (1756–1791)

K. 310

**Allegro maestoso**

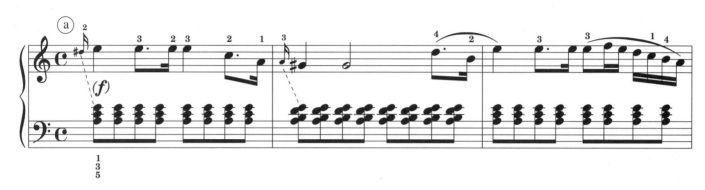

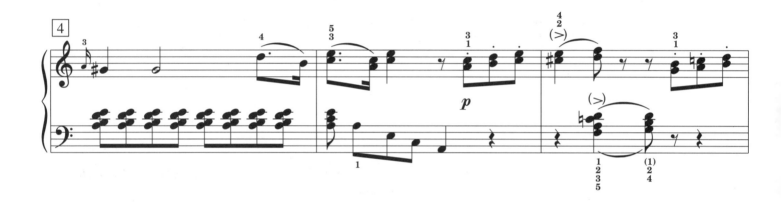

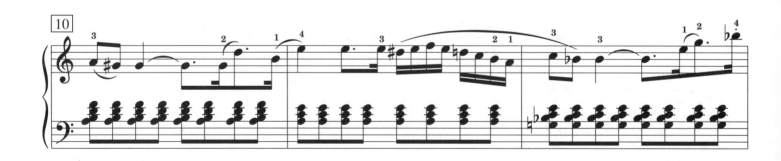

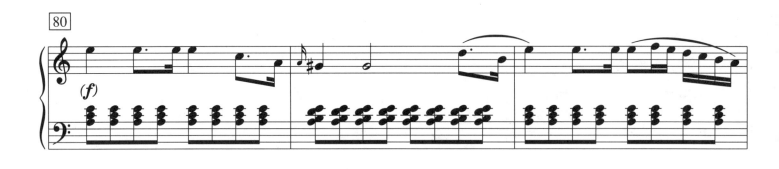

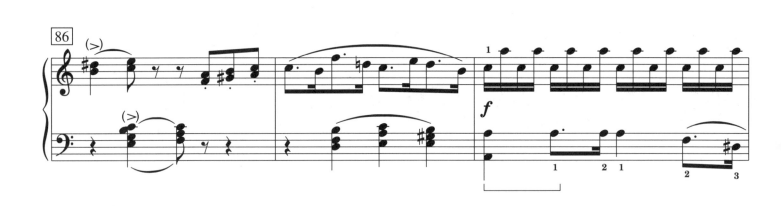

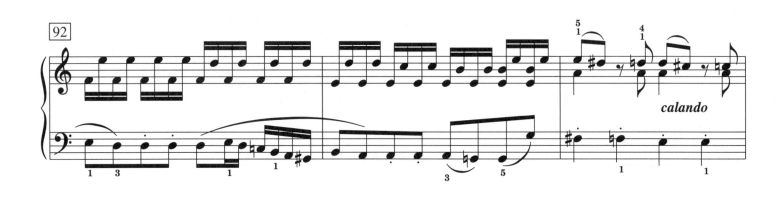

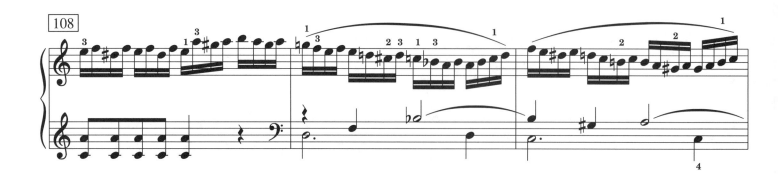

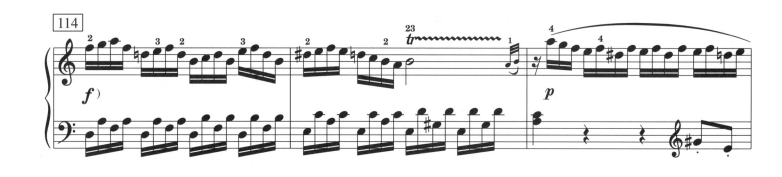

176

**Andante cantabile con espressione**

(a) Play the RH grace note expressively before the LH octave.

# Divertimento No. 6 in C Major

Josef Mysliveček
(1737–1781)

**Rondo**

(a) Dynamics and articulation are editorial.

D.C. al Fine

# Toccata in D Minor

Christian Gottlob Neefe
(1748–1798)

(a) Articulation is editorial.

194

# Minuet in C Major

Ignaz Joseph Pleyel
(1757–1831)

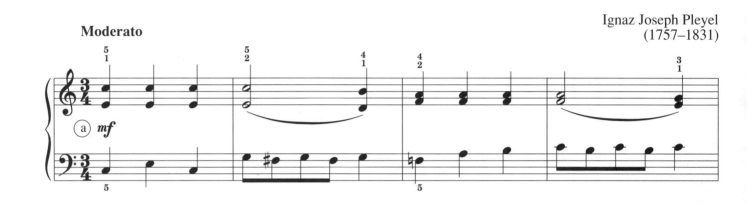

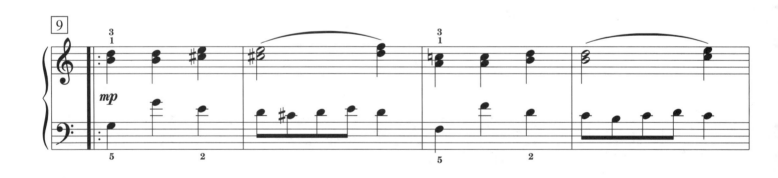

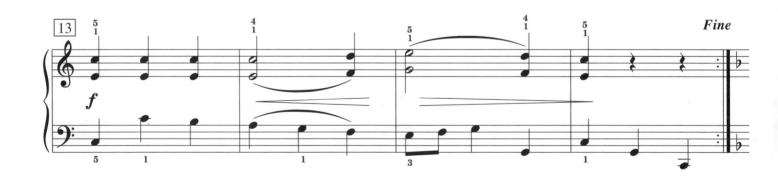

(a) Dynamics and articulation are editorial.

**Trio**

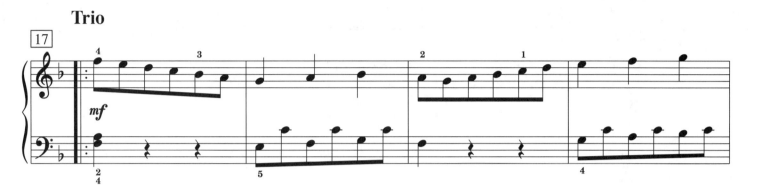

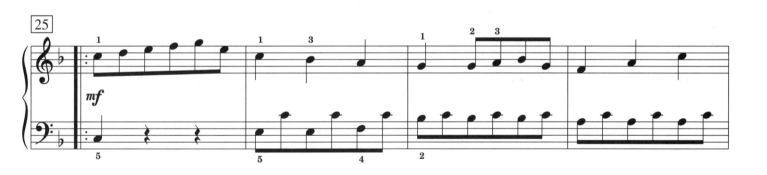

*D.C. al Fine*

# Rondo in G Major

Ignaz Joseph Pleyel
(1757–1831)

(a) Dynamics and articulation are editorial.

(b)

(c) Play the grace notes on the beat like crushed notes.

This editorial short cadenza could be enlarged within the measures with fermatas.

# Prelude in C Major

Johann Friedrich Reichardt
(1752–1814)

(a) Dynamics and articulation are editorial.

# Steer Her Up and Had Her Gawn

Alexander Reinagle
(1759–1809)

(a)   Dynamics and articulation are editorial.

**Variation II**

**Variation III**

**Variation IV**

# Trifle

Ferdinand Ries (1784–1838)
Op. 58, No. 12

208

## Trio I

**(Allegro)**

*D.C. Senza Replica
a poi il Trio II*
(Repeat measures 1–16,
then go to Trio II)

## Trio II

**(Allegretto grazioso)**

**D.C. al Fine**

# Five Écossaises

## I

Franz Schubert (1797–1828)
D. 299, No. 1

## II

D. 977, No. 7

# III

D. 735, No. 1

(Allegretto marcato)

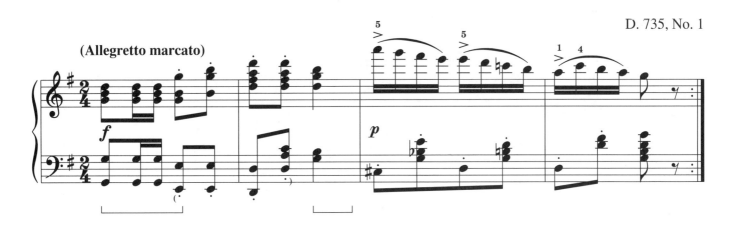

# IV

D. 735, No. 2

(Moderato grazioso)

# V

**(Con moto)** (a)

D. 783, No. 1

(a) Schubert ended the piece at measure 16. The editor has repeated measures 1–8 (17–24) to conclude in the opening tonic key of B minor.

# Two Ländler

## I

Franz Schubert (1797–1828)
D. 366, No. 3

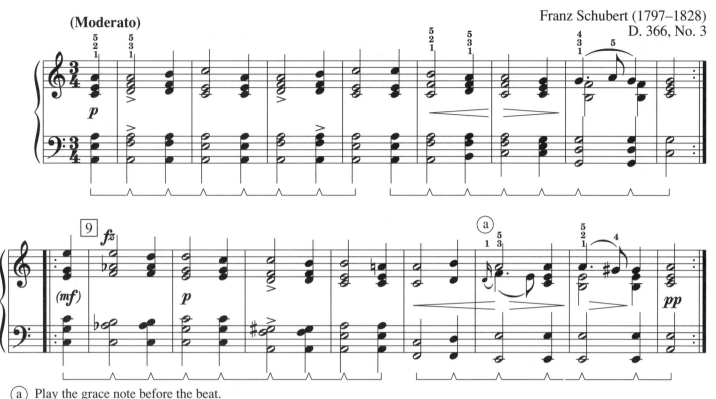

(a) Play the grace note before the beat.

## II

D. 366, No. 4

# German Dance in C Major

Franz Schubert (1797–1828)
D. 41, No. 20

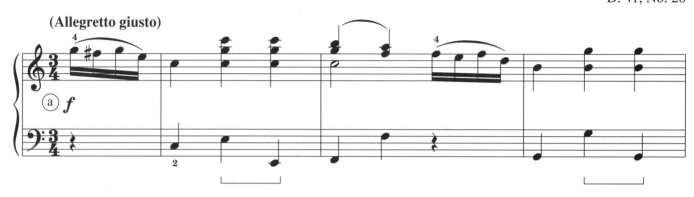

(a) Dynamics and articulation are editorial.

**Trio**

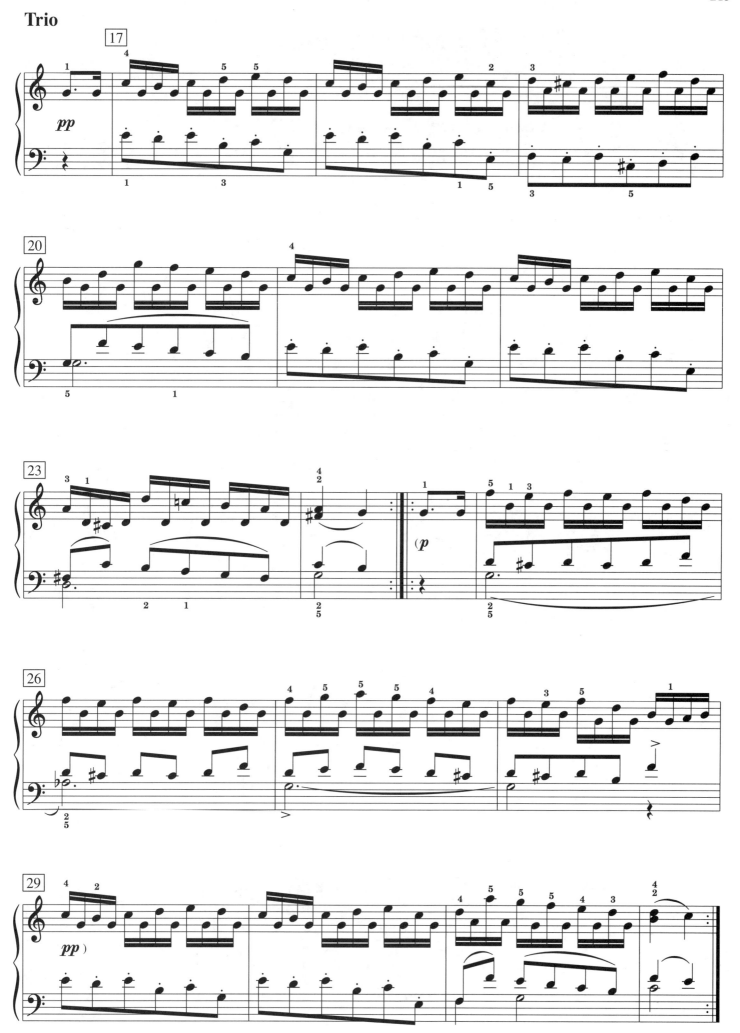

*D.C. al Fine*

# Hungarian Melody

Franz Schubert (1797–1828)
D. 817

(a) Play appoggiaturas slightly before the beat without an accent.

# Impromptu in A-flat Major

Franz Schubert (1797–1828)
Op. 142, No. 2; D. 935

**Trio**

# March in B Minor

Franz Schubert (1797–1828)
no Deutsch number

*March D.C. al Fine*

# Moments musicaux
## No. 3 in F Minor

Franz Schubert (1797–1828)
Op. 94, No. 3; D. 780, No. 3

(a) Play grace notes slightly before the beat.

# No. 6 in A-flat Major

Op. 94, No. 6; D. 780, No. 6

(a) Play grace notes slightly before the beat.

## Trio

*Allegretto D.C. al Fine*

# Rondo in G Major

Raynor Taylor
(1747–1825)

(a)   Dynamics and articulation are editorial.

# Sonatina in F Major

Daniel Gottlob Türk
(1750–1813)

# Three Écossaises

## I

Carl Maria von Weber (1786–1826)
(no opus number)

ⓐ Dynamics and articulation are editorial.

# II

Op. 4, No. 5

ⓐ Articulation is editorial.

# III

Op. 4, No. 6

(a) Play the grace note on the beat.

# Prelude in A Major

Samuel Wesley
(1766–1837)

(a) Dynamics and articulation are editorial.

(b) Play the grace note on the beat.

# Sonata in B-flat Major

Samuel Wesley (1766–1837)
Op. 5, No. 2

**Hornpipe**

(a) The dotted eighth and sixteenth note figure 𝅘𝅥𝅭𝅘𝅥𝅯 may be played 𝅘𝅥𝅭𝅘𝅥𝅯 throughout this movement.

(b) Dynamics and articulation are editorial.

# Waltz